Rise Above

A 90-Day Devotional

Other books in the Soul Surfer Series:

Soul Surfer Bible

Nonfiction:
Ask Bethany—FAQs: Surfing, Faith & Friends

Soul Surfer series

Rise Above

A 90-Day Devotional

Bethany Hamilton

with Doris Rikkers

zonder**kidz**

ZONDERVAN.com/
AUTHORTRACKER
follow your favorite authors

ZONDERKIDZ

Rise Above
Copyright © 2007 by Bethany Hamilton

This title is also available as a Zondervan ebook.
Visit www.zondervan.com/ebooks.

Requests for information should be addressed to:
Zonderkids, *Grand Rapids, Michigan 49530*

Library of Congress Cataloging-in-Publication Data

Hamilton, Bethany.
    Rise above : a 90 day devotional / written by Bethany Hamilton with Doris Rikkers.
       p. cm. — (Soul surfer series)
    Originally published: c2007.
    ISBN 978-0-310-72567-1 (softcover)
    1. Girls—Religious life—Juvenile literature. 2. Girls—Prayers and devotions I. Rikkers,
Doris. II. Title.
BV4551.3.H36 2011
242'.62—dc22   2010037917

Interior design: Christine Orejuela-Winkelman
Art direction and cover design: Merit Alderink

Printed in the United States of America

---

11 12 13 14 15 16 17 18 /DCI/ 18 17 16 15 14 13 12 11 10 9 8 7 6 5 4

Contents

About Bethany _____ 9

1 Big Plans Ahead _____ 10

2 Rock Solid Foundation _____ 12

3 Faithful Friends _____ 14

4 Who? Me? _____ 16

5 No Fear _____ 18

6 Close to Paradise _____ 20

7 Being Creative _____ 22

8 Music to My Ears _____ 24

9 Caring for Others _____ 26

10 Winning and Losing _____ 28

11 A Prayer for Help _____ 30

12 Passion Fruit _____ 32

13 Morning Wake Up _____ 34

14 Waiting for My Prince _____ 36

15 Walking on Water _____ 38

16 Never Too Young _____ 40

17 Keep Focused _____ 42

18 God's Beautiful Creation _____ 44

19 Talent Show _____ 46

20 What Should I Wear? _____ 48

21 Keep Smiling! _____ 50

22 What's Your Story? _____ 52

23 Every Place Is an Adventure _____ 54

24 Taking the Blame _____ 56

25 A Winning Prayer _____ 58

26 Twisting the Facts _____ 60

27 Doing the Impossible _____ 62

28 I Believe _____ 64

29 Mirror Images _____ 66

30 Outpouring of *Aloha* 68

31 Lasting Happiness 70

32 God, Tired? Not! 72

33 Service Center 74

34 What a Thrill! 76

35 For This I'm Thankful 78

36 Our Own Personal Cheerleader 80

37 We've Got Trouble 82

38 Dream a Little Dream 84

39 Getting an A for Attitude 86

40 Raindrops Keep Falling 88

41 How Strong Is God? 90

42 Popularity Isn't All That 92

43 Shine On 94

44 And You Are? 96

45 Take Time for God 98

46 Why Me? 100

47 Teeming Millions 102

48 Lots of Little Presents 104

49 Lots of Courage 106

50 Don't Just Believe It … Do It! 108

51 Jesus Is My Every Day 110

52 Don't Stress Out! 112

53 Running from God 114

54 Looking at the Inside 116

55 Oh, Yes You Can 118

56 The Best of Friends 120

57 Being a Winner 122

58 Living Temples 124

59 Speak Up 126

60 It's a Bummer 128

61 Sweet Sleeping 130

62 Good to the Finish 132

63 Something to Brag About _____ 134
64 The Problem Fixer _____ 136
65 Brain Food: No Junk Allowed _____ 138
66 The Guilt Dumpster _____ 140
67 Laugh a Lot _____ 142
68 The Body Machine _____ 144
69 A Day to Rejoice _____ 146
70 Obeying Parents _____ 148
71 A Special Kind of Kindness _____ 150
72 Being Responsible _____ 152
73 Faith for Now _____ 154
74 Willing Worship _____ 156
75 Like Talking to a Friend _____ 158
76 Giving Back to God _____ 160
77 No More Pity Party _____ 162
78 Stuff Happens _____ 164
79 Extra Helpers _____ 166
80 Everything Sings Praise _____ 168
81 Super Joy _____ 170
82 Mouth Checkup _____ 172
83 A Rainbow of Promises _____ 174
84 Mixed Messages _____ 176
85 Sticking Out _____ 178
86 Let's Be Honest _____ 180
87 We've Got the Power _____ 182
88 Armor of God _____ 184
89 Getting to Know You _____ 186
90 Into the Future _____ 188

About Bethany:

On a beautiful October morning in 2003, thirteen-year-old Bethany Hamilton woke up early, eager to start the day. The surf was up, and she wanted to join her friend Alana for a few hours of surfing off the North Shore of Kauai. While resting on her surfboard, waiting for the next perfect wave, Bethany caught a glimpse of a shadow moving in the water. She felt a tug on her left arm and then saw the blood. Without screaming or panicking, she quickly called out to her friends that she had been attacked by a shark.

Bethany's calmness, courage, and faith in God helped her to survive the trauma, face the pain of losing her arm, and move on with her life. Within weeks of the attack, she was back in the water surfing. Within months, she was competing in a surfing contest.

Bethany has used her experience to tell others about her faith and the loving God she serves. She is an inspiration to everyone who hears her story.

We hope that you find inspiration in Bethany's story of faith and love, and that you also find the courage to rise above.

Devotion 1
Big Plans Ahead

On that October morning of the shark attack, everyone around me (including me!) feared that my plans for being a professional surfer were over. Who had ever heard of a surfer with one arm? How would I paddle out? How would I get up on the board? How would I balance? All the hopes and dreams about surfing that I'd had since I was little seemed to be gone.

But you know what? God had plans for me. He had bigger plans than I could have ever imagined. Before the attack, I might have become a surfer and been well-known in the surfing crowd. I might have had my picture on several surfing magazines. But now God is able to use me in a different way, above and beyond all that I could ever ask or think. He's doing things in my life that I could never have dreamed of before the attack. He's helping me to rise above it all.

God has big plans for your life too. The purpose he has for your life is different than the one he has for mine. But he's got plans. Big plans. You need to be willing to be used by him. Trust him. Follow him. Ask him to start preparing your heart for his purpose.

God's Words Inspire

"For I know the plans I have for you," declares the L*ORD,* *"plans to prosper you and not to harm you, plans to give you hope and a future."*

—Jeremiah 29:11

Chatting with God

Dear God, thank you for having a plan for me. Help me to trust that your plan for my future is the best for me. Give me patience and help me to prepare for what you have in store for me. In Jesus' name, amen.

Did You Know?

Jeremiah 29:11 is one of my favorite Bible verses. My youth counselor, Sarah, was inspired by God to think of it the morning she heard about the attack. It's been a great support for me, my family, and my friends ever since.

Devotion 2
Rock Solid Foundation

I've spent my whole life enjoying the ocean, the surf, and the sand on the beach. I know all about sand castles and the surf. I've seen how one wave can just wipe out a sand castle in a second. Houses, castles, dreams, or plans only last if they are built on a solid foundation. God is the rock in my life—my foundation. I keep my relationship with him strong.

It's good to have dreams. I hope you have lots of dreams to do spectacular things. But you have to put your hope and faith into something that can't suddenly disappear. You need a strong foundation, a hard rock platform to build your dreams and future plans upon. Anything less than that will be a total wipeout.

Popularity can be lost with one round of gossip. Money can be easily taken away or lost. Clothes go out of style. Nothing really lasts except God's love. If you build your hopes and dreams and your life on him, you'll always be on solid ground and able to survive life's challenges.

God's Words Inspire

Therefore everyone who hears these words of mine and puts them into practice is like a wise man who built his house on the rock. The rain came down, the streams rose, and the winds blew and beat against that house; yet it did not fall, because it had its foundation on the rock.
                              —Matthew 7:24–5

Chatting with God

Jesus, help me to put my faith in you. Help me build my life upon you, my Rock, so I will be strong and secure in you. In Jesus' name, amen.

Did You Know?

Have you ever picked up a handful of sand and tried to count the grains? Have you noticed all the different color variations and seen how it sparkles when the sun shines on it? It's made from the earth's elements of the area it's in: coral, shells, rock, sandstone, quartz, etc. There are even beaches with all black sand from volcanic rock. How precious are God's thoughts toward us that they are more in number than the grains of sand on the beach (Psalm 139:17–18).

Devotion 3
Faithful Friends

One of the greatest gifts God has given me is my friends. One of my dearest friends is Alana, my surfing buddy. Alana was surfing with me when I got attacked by the shark. She stayed with me through the whole thing. She's awesome!

I have a big *ohana* of friends too: friends from my church, friends from the community, and friends from the surfing world. Then there's my tight group of personal friends. These are the friends who will love me no matter what. They loved me with two arms, and they love me now with one arm. My friends have been the greatest to help me through the tough times. They've made me laugh and feel normal again.

God wants us to be Christlike in our relationships with our friends. He wants us to be a friend others can trust and receive encouragement from—not condemnation or criticism. Jesus is the best friend you could ever have. He wants only what is best for us. He gives us guidance in his Word for our safety and protection. He promises to never leave us or forsake us. Real friends are like Jesus. They shine with Jesus' love. I hope you will be a friend like that.

God's Words Inspire

A friend loves at all times.
            —Proverbs 17:17

Chatting with God

Dear Jesus, thank you for being my very best friend. Thank you for the friends I have in my life right now. Help me to be a faithful friend whom others can trust. Help me to be a friend who forgives, encourages, loves, and laughs with others. In Jesus' name, amen.

Did You Know?

Ohana is a Hawaiian word that means "family unit or close group."

Devotion 4
Who? Me?

There's a story in the Old Testament about God calling Moses to lead his people out of Egypt. Moses can't believe that God would call him for the job. He gives God all kinds of excuses: *Who, me? What if they don't believe you sent me? I don't know what to say* (Exodus 3–4). I get where Moses was at. Since the attack, loads of people want to interview me, take my picture, or write another article about the shark attack. Before the attack, I had been asking God to use me to glorify him. I realized pretty early on that this was a chance for me to be God's voice. I still get nervous when I hear that: God's voice. Who, me? That's crazy! What if I blow it? And I do sometimes, especially if I can't think of what to say—I call it *mind blank*. But then, I just pray and ask God for help. This is what God wants me to do for him right now. So I use every chance I get to tell others about God's goodness, peace, and love. I don't mind being in the spotlight so much when I get to give God all the glory!

God is calling you too. He may want you to be his voice. He may want you to be his hands, helping a neighbor. God can use you in small ways and big ways. The important thing is that you are ready to answer, "Here I am. Use me."

God's Words Inspire

Moses said to the LORD, "O Lord, I have never been eloquent, neither in the past nor since you have spoken to your servant. I am slow of speech and tongue." The LORD said to him, "Who gave man his mouth? Is it not I, the LORD? Now go; I will help you speak and will teach you what to say."
—Exodus 4:10–12

Chatting with God

Lord Jesus, thank you for every opportunity you've given me to talk about you! I want to be used by you today somehow. Show me what I can do to share your love, and give me the ability to go and do it. In Jesus' name, amen.

Did You Know?

I've been able to talk about God on *Inside Edition, The Early Show, Good Morning America, The Today Show, Oprah, 20/20,* MTV's *TRL,* and at the *Teen Choice Awards* (to name a few). Thank God for those opportunities!

Devotion 5
No Fear

What are you afraid of? What makes you freeze up with fear? What gives you that creepy, shivery feeling all over?

Slithering snakes?

Big hairy spiders? (I think those are creepy!)

Booming thunderstorms?

A growling dog?

Speaking in front of the class?

Wearing a bathing suit?

Whenever I speak about how I lost my arm, people always ask how I'm not afraid of the water or sharks. To tell you the truth, I am afraid of sharks. I get spooked when I think I see a shadow under the water. But my passion for surfing outweighs my fears of unseen danger. I'm not so afraid that I would never go surfing again.

Most of the time, though, I don't focus on fear. I choose to concentrate on the good things and put my trust in God's care. I'm not really afraid, because I have a very *big* God by my side. Even though bad things may happen to you, God is still there with you and can use that bad thing for a good purpose. If you have God by your side, you don't have to be afraid either. God will give you the strength to face whatever scares you.

God's Words Inspire

Be strong and courageous. Do not be terrified; do not be discouraged, for the LORD your God will be with you wherever you go.
—Joshua 1:9

Chatting with God

Oh God, help me to remember that you are always by my side, no matter what I have to face. Keep me strong and courageous as I trust in you. In Jesus' name, amen.

Did You Know?

It is very rare for a shark to attack a person. There's a better chance that a strange dog on the street will bite you than that a shark will attack you.

Devotion 6
Close to Paradise

Hawaii is the only home I've ever known.
I've visited a lot of places on the mainland
and in other parts of the world, but I'm hap-
piest when I come home. Hawaii has great
waves, warm water, beautiful people, and fresh
bananas and papayas. I like to pick papayas
and bananas from the trees in my yard to make
smoothies.

When I look around me and see how beautiful
this island is, I wonder if this is what the garden of
Eden was like. Hawaii has everything: lush tropical
rain forests, waterfalls, volcanoes, beautiful beaches,
rocky coasts, and steep cliffs. It's definitely my idea
of paradise.

God places each of us where we are for a purpose. I know that he wants me to be who I am
right here in Hawaii. He has put you in Maine
or Ohio, Texas or California, or Canada for
a purpose too. We each have to find out
what God wants us to do and then do it.
Oh, but now that I think about
it—there is one big difference

between Hawaii and the original garden of Eden—we don't have snakes!

God's Words Inspire

Go into all the world and preach the good news to all creation.
                              —Mark 16:15

Chatting With God

Dear God, thank you for giving me a home. I know you have a purpose for me here to share your good news. Help me to seek that purpose and not miss it—so others may experience your peace in their relationships. In Jesus' name, amen.

Did You Know?

Kauai is the name of the Hawaiian island that I live on. It's the one that's farthest to the north in the chain of islands that make up the state of Hawaii. Until recently, the Alakai Swamp on Mount Waialeale in Kauai was thought to be the wettest place on earth. And boy does it rain here!

Devotion 7
Being Creative

Most people love to walk along the sandy beaches of the ocean and enjoy the sound of the crashing waves. And then they bend over and pick up a seashell, like they can't stop themselves from doing it. Some places have really cool seashells, others have rather ordinary ones. My friends and I often enjoy hunting for shells that wash up along the beach. This is one of the things we do when the ocean's flat and calm and we can't surf. Then on rainy days when there isn't much else to do we sit around and get creative with our beach treasures—shells, glass, seeds, and other miscellaneous treasures—turning them into earrings, necklaces, mirror frames ... anything we can think of!

I really like to create things. I especially like to make stuff from the shells I've collected. But I need *something* to start with, like shells and glue and something to put them on. Whenever I think about God creating the world from scratch, I'm blown away. To take nothing and make this world from it; I can't even begin to understand how he did it. But I believe God's proven Word and know that God is all powerful and can do anything. What an awesome God we have!

God's Words Inspire

In the beginning God created the heavens and the earth. Now the earth was formless and empty, darkness was over the surface of the deep, and the Spirit of God was hovering over the waters. And God said, "Let there be light," and there was light.

—Genesis 1:1–3

Chatting with God

Almighty God, Creator of everything, thank you for this beautiful world that you made. I praise you for all that you are and for all that you are doing in my life. I thank you for caring about me and for loving me. As the morning sun rises, help me start each day fresh in your love and forgiveness. In Jesus' name, amen.

Did You Know?

Sunrise shells are rare and hard to find. They are pink, orange, and yellow: the colors of the sunrise, and are the most stunning shell that you can find on Kauai.

Devotion 8
Music to My Ears

Music is one of the most powerful tools in the world that can influence people's lives. I like to listen to music that encourages good things in my life. Our car CD player is always loaded with praise and worship CDs and contemporary Christian artists. Not only do they have good music, but they also include lyrics that speak of Jesus and God's love. Praising God is a part of my everyday life.

The church I attend really enjoys praise and worship. We sing a lot of contemporary songs, but we also sing favorite traditional songs and Hawaiian hymns—all in praise to God. Sometimes when I'm sitting out on my board in the water, I am so inspired by the beauty that I can't help but make up new worship songs to the Lord.

Singing praise to God is important for all of us. Here are a few reasons why I praise God: He paid a price we could not pay. He died on the cross after a sinless life. He completely forgives all our sins. His love for each and every one of us is unconditional. He created us, cares for us and provides for us.

The important thing is that the praise comes from your heart!

God's Words Inspire

Sing to him a new song; play skillfully, and shout for joy. For the word of God is right and true; he is faithful in all he does.
                    —Psalm 33:3–4

Chatting with God

Lord, you are worthy of praise. Your mercies are new every morning. Help me to live today giving mercy and forgiveness and love to others. In Jesus' name, amen.

Did You Know?

Psalm 47:1 says, "Clap your hands all you peoples!" Now that I have one arm, I can't really clap my hands to the music. But I can never lose my ability to worship God!

Devotion 9
Caring for Others

People think that I must be sad because I only have one arm. But that doesn't make me sad at all—I'm thankful to be alive and still have one arm! What makes me sad is seeing people who are in need of Jesus or who are rejected by others.

When I was in New York City to show up on talk shows, I saw homeless people. Everybody else just ignored them—walked right past them and didn't help. I couldn't keep walking. I stopped by a homeless girl in the subway and gave her my coat. I wish I could have done more. The people I was with (those from a TV station) all thought this was such a big deal. I guess they have gotten used to ignoring these people. It wasn't a big deal for me. I was only doing what Jesus would do. When Jesus was here on earth he said, "When you do good to the least of these you do it to me." This homeless girl fell into that category of "the least of these." I just was helping out, like Jesus would. We can all help others. You can help too, no matter how old you are. You can help feed those who are hungry in your community by donating food. You can collect or donate clothes that you no longer wear. You can share your lunch or bring a smile to a neighbor who is sick. Any gift given in the name of Jesus, large or small, is doing what Jesus would do.

God's Words Inspire

For I was hungry and you gave me something to eat, I was thirsty and you gave me something to drink, I was a stranger and you invited me in, I needed clothes and you clothed me, I was sick and you looked after me, I was in prison and you came to visit me.
—Matthew 25:35–36

Chatting with God

Dear God, help me to be generous; give me compassion for the people you love so much. Help me to notice others who are in need and to not turn away. Put in me the desire to reach out to them and help them. In Jesus' name, amen.

Did You Know?

I work with World Vision, raising money for disabled children around the world. There are more than one hundred million disabled children in the world. Many of them are rejected by their families and society.

Devotion 10
Winning and Losing

Surfing is a big part of my life. I believe
I was born to surf. My family claims that I
have salt water in my veins! Not only do I love
to surf, I love to compete in surfing competitions. I started surfing competitions right when I
started surfing, so I've never really *not* competed.
I suppose I'm so competitive because I have two
older brothers. I've always wanted to show them
that I could do almost anything as good, or better,
than they could. When the surf is big, some kids get
intimidated by the size of the waves. Me? I live for it!
Six-foot swells get me stoked!

Surfing is a rush. Every time I catch a wave, I
challenge myself to do my best. So I'm always
competing with myself. When my friends and I
are in an official competition, we all try to do
our best. When one of us wins, we all win. And
we've all had our turn at losing too.

After all these years, I've learned that
sooner or later you're going to fall—even
in competition—so you might as well
learn from your mistakes and move
forward. The advice my dad

always gives me is, "Don't get upset or sore. There'll always be another opportunity to show you can do it. It's over. Move on."

There's nothing wrong with being competitive. There's nothing wrong with wanting to win. What's more important is attempting to do your best. And if today is not your day to win, there will always be a next time. So stay positive and humble, practice consistently with a good attitude, and be willing to try again.

God's Words Inspire

When pride comes, then comes disgrace, but with humility comes wisdom.
        —Proverbs 11:2

Chatting with God

Dear God, help me to have a good attitude, even when I make mistakes and fall. Keep me humble; don't let me be too proud or full of myself. Help me to always have good relationships with friends and competitors, so that I may always bring you glory. In Jesus' name, amen.

Did You Know?

Stoked is a surfer's slang term that means "excited."

Devotion 11
A Prayer for Help

The attack happened so fast that, after calling for help, I knew it was time for serious prayer. As Alana's dad, Holt, took control of the situation and paddled me in, he told me to talk out loud so he would know that I was still conscious. So I *prayed* out loud. Everybody helped to get me to the beach. With Alana by my side, I clung on to Holt's board shorts and prayed desperately, "Please God, help me. God, let me get to the beach." It was a long quarter of a mile to the beach, and it took us twenty minutes to get to shore, where I knew I would get help and be safe.

I usually consider all my prayers urgent—like right now: "Please help me on this test." "Please let so-and-so like me." "Please don't let me look like a goof in front of the class," or (in my case) "... on national TV!" We pray for big things and little things. We pray for ourselves and for others. God cares about every detail. He listens to our prayers no matter how short or long they are. He listens to our hearts, so even if he wouldn't give us an A for English, he knows what we're trying to say.

Sometimes God answers prayer immediately. He did for me in my particular situation. Sometimes he takes a little longer. Sometimes his answer is "no." Because he knows what's good for us, he will only give us what will make us stronger. Our job is to trust and to have faith and believe that he will answer in the way that is best for us. Then we wait patiently and see what God will do.

God's Words Inspire

This is the confidence we have in approaching God: if we ask anything according to his will, he hears us.
—1 John 5:14

Chatting with God

Dear Lord, thank you for letting me talk to you any time I need to. I praise you for being a God who loves me and always listens, even to my smallest needs. In Jesus' name, amen.

Did You Know?

Pule is the Hawaiian word for "prayer."

Devotion 12
Passion Fruit

One of the things that I love about living in Hawaii is its fresh tropical fruit. Two of my favorite fruits are bananas and papayas. We even grow them in my backyard. Yogurt and granola with sliced bananas on top and sprinkled with cinnamon is so tasty! But my favorite fruit is passion fruit, or lilikoi.

The Holy Spirit has special kinds of "fruit" called the fruit of the Spirit. They are love, joy, peace, patience, kindness, goodness, faithfulness, gentleness, and self-control. If we are filled with the Holy Spirit and God's love, we will show off these "fruits" to other people in the way we live and talk. The Bible tells us that we should "live a life worthy of the Lord and ... please him in every way: bearing fruit in every good work, growing in the knowledge of God" (Colossians 1:10).

We can show that Jesus lives in our hearts. We can share our lunch or help a friend with homework. We can tell someone she did a good job. We can listen to someone's problem and then not gossip about it. Sometimes it means we don't brag about what we have or what we've done. All that we do and say and even think should show that we are full of God's Spirit.

God's Words Inspire

But the fruit of the Spirit is love, joy, peace, patience, kindness, goodness, faithfulness, gentleness and self-control.
—Galatians 5:22–23

Chatting with God

Dear Lord, thank you for sending your Spirit to live in me. I want my life to bear spiritual fruit. Help me to show others that I am filled with your love by everything I say and everything I do. In Jesus' name, amen.

Did You Know?

Papaia is the Hawaiian word for "papaya." Not only is it one of the most popular fruits eaten in Hawaii, it's also used for medicine and to tenderize meat.

Devotion 13
Morning Wake Up

My daily schedule usually revolves around the surf. I wake up at around seven a.m. and, after checking the buoy report, head to the beach (if it looks like there are waves). As you know, I'm an avid surf nut. Surfing is what I like to do more than anything else. When the surf's really pounding, I can hear it from my house, and it's a sure way of getting me out of bed!

Sometimes I have devotions and spend some time with God in the morning before I get out of bed. Other times, we head straight for the beach. I really enjoy the quiet of the morning and watching the sun come up (if I get up extra early). That's a good time to talk to God. It's peaceful out there, a great place to be alone with God and experience the beauty of his creation: the birds, the water, the sky, the sun, and the waves.

Spending time with God is the best way to start your day. You can spend quiet time with God no matter where you live. Even if your morning is crazy, find some time in your day to be alone with God and to listen for his words to you.

God's Words Inspire

*In the morning, O LORD, you hear my voice;
in the morning I lay my requests before you and
wait in expectation.*
—Psalm 5:3

Chatting with God

Dear God, thank you for each new day and the morning sunrise. Take care of me and my family and friends all day long. Guide me to do things that will please you. Help me to show your love to others through this day. In Jesus' name, amen.

Did You Know?

A *surf nut* is someone who is crazy about surfing (like me and my friends!).

Devotion 14
Waiting for My Prince

Some girls want to marry a perfect prince.
Think of Cinderella, who was kind, patient, and
unselfish. When she met the prince, she knew
right away that they were meant for each other.
He could see her pure heart. She could see he was
worth waiting for. I'm not interested in having a boy-
friend. I'm waiting for my prince.

For now, I'll spend my time doing what I love,
what I'm called by God to do. I have loads of friends
to hang out with. The group of girls that I hang out
and surf with is always doing fun, crazy stuff. Sure,
there are boys in my youth group at church and
boys I know from surfing and competitions, but
all of us just hang out together and have fun
with no pressure.

The media hypes us up to think that we
need a serious relationship with boys, but
I would rather wait for God's perfect
will. I know that when the time is
right, God will bring the right guy

to me. In the meantime I want to enjoy what I have, not focus on what I don't have.

God's Words Inspire

Promise me, O women of Jerusalem, by the swift gazelles and the deer of the wild, not to awaken love until the time is right.
—Song of Solomon 2:7 (NLT)

Chatting with God

Dear Lord, help me to enjoy my life right now. Help me to trust you with my future. Give me patience to accept that you know what's best for me and that you will put everything in place in my life when it's time. In Jesus' name, amen.

Did You Know?

In the surfing world, *groms* are kids who surf.

Devotion 15
Walking on Water

I have a favorite Bible story ... actually, I have a whole bunch of them! But the one that's my very favorite is the story about Jesus walking on the water. After a busy day, Jesus sent the disciples off in their boat. There were big waves and lots of wind out on the middle of the lake. The disciples were in a fishing boat, scared to death. Then Jesus showed up in the middle of the storm. At first the disciples thought he was a ghost or something. They thought he was still on the land. Not only was he out there on the lake, he was walking on the water!

I love the waves and the water. Riding a wave is my favorite sensation. Jesus tops that though—he walks on water like he's walking on solid ground. I've seen what the ocean does in a storm. It's not very safe to be out in the water when the surf gets huge, scary, and unpredictable. But Jesus calmly walked out on the water to the frightened disciples, telling them not to be afraid.

When we walk with Jesus, we walk with a God who is more

powerful than the biggest wave in the sea, the strongest wind or storm, or our greatest fear. We can be courageous because God is by our side.

God's Words Inspire

During the fourth watch of the night Jesus went out to them, walking on the lake. When the disciples saw him walking on the lake, they were terrified. "It's a ghost," they said, and cried out in fear. But Jesus immediately said to them: "Take courage! It is I. Don't be afraid."

—Matthew 14:25–27

Chatting with God

Almighty God, thank you for being more powerful than any force of nature. Thank you for protecting me. Give me good judgment and wisdom to avoid dangerous situations. Help me to have courage and to not be afraid no matter what I face. In Jesus' name, amen.

Did You Know?

The biggest wave ever recorded was 1,720 feet high (tsunami in Lituya Bay, Alaska, 1958).

Devotion 16
Never Too Young

So often young people think they can't do anything for God because they are too young, too little, not smart enough, not wise enough, not a good speaker, or whatever. There are just loads of excuses. But you know what? God can use you right here, right now. Hey, I was just thirteen when that shark attacked me. And presto! Within days I was telling people all over the world that Jesus saved me.

At first all that attention was weird. But after a while, I came to realize that it's pretty amazing. If God wants me to have all this attention, then I need to put the focus on him. I can then tell people that God is the one who saved me. God is the one who deserves the attention and the praise for keeping me alive through the attack.

God is in control of my life and yours. Even though we might be young, he can use us to tell others about his love. You can tell others about God's love for you at home, in your neighborhood, at your school, and with your friends. You can start now. You don't have to wait.

God's Words Inspire

Don't let anyone look down on you because you are young, but set an example for the believers in speech, in life, in love, in faith and in purity.

—1 Timothy 4:12

Chatting with God

Dear Lord, I know I am young, but you can use me to set a good example and be a witness for you. Show me how to do this. Give me the opportunity and courage to share your truth with others, especially with my peers. In Jesus' name, amen.

Did You Know?

Dawn patrol is a term for rising early to search for waves.

Devotion 17
Keep Focused

In surfing, it is very important that you
are constantly aware and focused, that you
never let your guard down. Here is my advice
for surfers or in whatever you do.

Be aware. When paddling out to surf, you
have to be aware of many things: the ocean
currents, tides, and channels, where the rocks
are, how large the set waves are, how many other
people are in the water, where the waves are breaking, and the reef or sandbar conditions.

Stay focused. When you're standing up to ride a
wave, you need to be completely focused in order
to enjoy your ride and not wipe out! It's happened
more than once that I got distracted by chatting
with my friends and I missed a really good wave.

Just like we miss those great waves, we also
miss some great opportunities sent our way
by God. The opportunities roll right by us
because we aren't paying attention to what
he is doing.

Are you focused on God and aware
of the opportunities he sends you? I
encourage you to focus on God's

overall plan, reach out to others (like people at your school), and be aware of the opportunities that he has for you.

God's Words Inspire

Let us fix our eyes on Jesus, the author and perfecter of our faith.
—Hebrews 12:2

Chatting with God

Dear God, thank you for giving me encouraging and wise advice in the Bible. Help me to be focused on your purpose and aware of what you're doing here on earth. Help me to also be aware of the opportunities that you give me everyday to live like Jesus and be a witness for you. In Jesus' name, amen.

Did You Know?

Surfers put wax on the deck, the top of the surfboard, so they can stand and ride a wave without slipping off.

Devotion 18
God's Beautiful Creation

I'm in awe of God and his creation. I spend a lot of time in the ocean, and I'm always amazed when I encounter God's beautiful creatures of the sea. Sea turtles and colorful fish swim under my board while I'm waiting to catch a wave. In the winter you can spot a huge whale leaping in the distance. And the dolphins like to show off early in the morning. Just like it says in Genesis, the waters teem with life. But a lot of people never get to see that stuff in person.

The land and water in your part of the world might be a bit different than mine, but they are still part of God's wonderful creation. And he has given it all to us as a gift to live in, to love, and to take care of.

I always try to encourage people to respect and care for God's beautiful creatures and the places he created for us to live. It's really pretty simple. We shouldn't litter. We should preserve what already exists. We should recycle or reuse stuff whenever we can. It's God's creation, but he put us in charge of it. Let's make sure it stays beautiful.

God's Words Inspire

And God said, "Let the water teem with living creatures, and let birds fly above the earth across the expanse of the sky." So God created the great creatures of the sea and every living and moving thing with which the water teems, according to their kinds, and every winged bird according to its kind. And God saw that it was good.
—Genesis 1:20–21

Chatting with God

Almighty God, thank you for your creation of the land, the ocean, and all the creatures that live there. Inspire me to always care for the land and the animals that you designed. In Jesus' name, amen.

Did You Know?

Hawaii's state fish is the Humuhumunukunukuapua'a (pronounced HOO-moo-HOO-moo-NOO-koo-NOO-koo-AH-poo-AH-ah). This means "fish with a pig's nose." In English, we call it the Triggerfish.

Devotion 19
Talent Show

All of us have some talent. I have friends that are good at math. Others are great at getting up in front of the class and giving a speech. A lot of my friends are good at sports. And there's always that friend who's really good at being a friend. You might not know yet what your real talent is. That's okay, just keep trying new things and praying for God to help you find that treasure of talent buried deep within you.

With practice, most of us can become good at more than one thing. I really love sports and music. When I was younger, I learned to play the guitar. I practiced every day and played for fun with my friends. Now that I can't do that, I play music on my iPod instead. I train and practice all the time to increase my skills in surfing. I believe that God has given me this talent as a gift. Right now, because I continued surfing with one arm after surviving a shark attack, I also have the opportunity to tell others about my faith in Jesus Christ.

The whole point of God gifting us with talent is so we can use it for his glory. If we all do our best at what we have a talent for, we'll make God's world a better place. Like in the parable of the talents, I hope one day to hear Jesus say to me, "Well done, good and faithful servant!" (Matthew 25:21).

God's Words Inspire

Whatever you do, do it all for the glory of God.

—1 Corinthians 10:31

Chatting with God

Dear Lord, thank you for each of the talents you have given me and my friends. It's awesome to see how these talents work together for your plan. Help me to honor you with everything you have given me. In Jesus' name, amen.

Did You Know?

Heenalu is the Hawaiian word meaning "to surf."

Devotion 20
What Should
I Wear?

What should I wear? What's in style? What should I shop for? These are all typical concerns girls have. Here in Hawaii, my wardrobe is rather simple. I wear a bathing suit, a sarong or shorts, and a tank top most of the time. This can bother my mom sometimes; she thinks that I shouldn't spend my whole day in a bathing suit.

I haven't counted in a while, but I probably own over three dozen bathing suits. I know that sounds like a lot, but my sponsor, Rip Curl, keeps me well supplied with bathing suits and clothes.

God's Word reminds us that he will take care of our basic needs. We just can't let clothes and how we look be too important to us or take up too much of our time. There are better things that God wants us to spend time on. Jesus says to focus on living a lifestyle that pleases him, and he will take care of everything else.

God's Words Inspire

So do not worry, saying, "What shall we eat?" or "What shall we drink?" or "What shall we wear?" For … your heavenly Father knows that you need them. But seek first his kingdom and his righteousness, and all these things will be given to you as well.
—Matthew 6:31–33

Chatting with God

Dear Heavenly Father, thank you for loving me and for always providing for my family and me. Help me to stay focused on who I am in you, not what I wear and how I look. Guide me in finding a way to put you and your Kingdom first before everything else that comes into my life. In Jesus' name, amen.

Did You Know?

A *sarong* is a loose skirt made of a long sheet of cloth that is wrapped around the body.

Devotion 21
Keep Smiling!

People are often surprised that I'm always smiling. I suppose they think I should be sad and have a bad attitude because I only have one arm. But that's the opposite of what God says. God has always been good to me. I'm still very much alive after a horrible attack, when I could have died. I can still do just about everything I could when I had two arms (okay, so buttons, cutting food, and shoelaces are a problem). But I can still surf! And most importantly, I can still serve God!

Everybody has problems in life. Some kids are poor and hungry. Some kids are sick. Others have only a mom or a dad, not both. Some have had accidents that cause them to be in a wheelchair. Everybody's got something that they're not happy about. But things should be different for Christians. We can pray about it! And even if we have problems or pain, we can be joyful in that we have God's love.

God knows what's best for my life. It makes me happy to know that he cares about me, my friends, and my family. The Bible says to "be joyful always"—and I can! Because no matter what happens—good or bad—I can call upon his name anytime! He will always be there to support me.

God's Words Inspire

A happy heart makes the face cheerful.
—Proverbs 15:13

Chatting with God

Dear God, thank you for coming into my heart and filling my life with joy. Help me to be brave to show others why I am happy. Help me to know the right words to say to tell them about you and the joy that you bring to my life. I want them to experience your kingdom of peace and joy and righteousness. In Jesus' name, amen.

Did You Know?

Minoaka is the Hawaiian word for "smile."

Devotion 22
What's Your Story?

We all have a story. Even when you're a kid, you have a story: where you were born, what your family is like, what you like to do. All those things make up your story.

Everybody thinks my story is awesome. They all say, "Wow, you have a story that's unbelievable. My life is dull compared to yours." Well, you know what? You have an exciting story too! For some of us (like me) the action and excitement happen in the first few chapters. Maybe in your life you're still in the introduction to the book. You never know what will happen in the next couple of chapters or at the end of the book. Crazy, huh? One turn of the page and BAM!, the excitement could begin.

In the Bible, Jesus chose fishermen to be his disciples. Maybe those guys thought their lives were a little dull. They would go out in their boat day after day and catch fish. Then one day Jesus came up to them and said, "Come, follow me ... and I will make you fishers of men"

(Matthew 4:19). Their lives were completely different after that.

If you make Jesus part of your story, it's bound to be exciting. Trust God to lead you through your life. Respond to him. He's got a perfect story in mind for you.

God's Words Inspire

Trust in the LORD with all your heart and lean not on your own understanding; in all your ways acknowledge him, and he will make your paths straight.
—Proverbs 3:5–6

Chatting with God

Oh Lord, I praise you for caring about me and wanting to be part of my story. Help me to enjoy my own life and not be envious of others. Help me to trust in you every day, even when things get dull. In Jesus' name, amen.

Did You Know?

A soul surfer is someone who surfs for the pure pleasure and joy of it.

Devotion 23
Every Place Is an Adventure

In the letters and emails I get, girls say, "Wow, you're so lucky to live in Hawaii. It would be such a fun place to live. Where I live is dull and boring." Well, you know what? Life can be an adventure no matter where you live. If you open up your eyes to your surroundings, you'll find lots of neat stuff to do and see—no matter where you live.

If you live in a place that gets snow, that's something special. I don't get to go skiing or snowboarding here in Hawaii. Or maybe you live in an exciting big city. Maybe you live near a lake or some mountains. Maybe you have lots of shopping malls nearby. The island of Kauai doesn't have any big shopping malls or skyscrapers. So, you see, every place has some advantages.

God has placed us wherever we are for a purpose. He wants us to be happy in that place, to discover the good stuff about it. Tons of people come to Hawaii on vacation every year. But you know what? Hawaiians usually go someplace else for their vacations. Look around you. What are the best things about living where you live? Find adventure right where you are. God wants you to enjoy it.

God's Words Inspire

I have learned the secret of being content in any and every situation, whether well fed or hungry, whether living in plenty or in want. I can do everything through him who gives me strength.
— Philippians 4:12–13

Chatting with God

Dear God, thank you for my home. Open my eyes to all the wonderful things that are around me. Help me to see that wherever I am I can find adventure and happiness. Show me how to be content with what I have and where I am. In Jesus' name, amen.

Did You Know?

Hawaii is known as the Aloha State. Of the fifty states, it is the only state that is surrounded by water on all sides.

Devotion 24
Taking the Blame

Did you ever do something wrong and get away with it? I'm sure everybody has. But have you ever had someone else get blamed for what you did? It can leave you feeling all mixed up inside. Part of you is glad that you didn't get caught. Another part of you feels guilty because the other person shouldn't have to take the blame. And another part of you is thankful.

Well, Jesus took the blame for us in a big way. When he died on the cross for us, he took the blame for all our sins. He did this because he loves us way more than any regular friend can. When he was on earth, Jesus told his disciples, "Greater love has no one than this, that he lay down his life for his friends. You are my friends if you do what I command" (John 15:13–14). He was giving them a hint that he was going to die for them.

Jesus died for everyone in the whole world: people who lived then, people who live now, and all people who will live in the future. He took the blame and the punishment for everybody. I know of a few friends who might take the blame for me if I did something dumb, but to die in my place? That's pretty awesome! I'm glad he's my friend.

God's Words Inspire

For God so loved the world that he gave his one and only Son, that whoever believes in him shall not perish but have eternal life.
—John 3:16

Chatting with God

Dear God, thank you for Jesus. Thank you for loving us so much that you sent him to take the blame and punishment for all of our sins. Help us to follow his commands to show that we are his friends. In Jesus' name, amen.

Did You Know?

Hoaloha is one of the ways to say "friend" in Hawaiian.

Devotion 25
A Winning Prayer

People who don't know me well sometimes think that I pray so I will win. I guess
they think I ask God to make me win. But I
don't. God doesn't work like that. We have to
do our part too. In sports we need to eat right,
take care of our bodies, work out, stay strong, and
practice, practice, practice.

You can't think that the first time you try something (kick a soccer ball, get up on a surfboard, or
ride a horse) you'll do it perfectly. Everybody knows
that people who place first in a competition have
dedicated a huge part of their lives to getting to
that goal.

I always pray before a surfing competition,
but I don't pray to win. I ask God to keep everyone safe and to help us all surf our best. I pray
that he will give me wisdom to know how
to position myself and to how to pick the
right wave to ride. I know I might wipe
out—that's part of the sport.

God will allow what is best for us
according to his overall plan. He's

got it all planned out. Sometimes that means winning and sometimes not.

God's Words Inspire

For the eyes of the Lord are on the righteous and his ears are attentive to their prayer.
—1 Peter 3:12

Chatting with God

Dear Lord, thank you for always listening to my prayers. Forgive me for sometimes being selfish in my prayers and my thoughts. Help me to seek and pray for what will bring you honor. In Jesus' name, amen.

Did You Know?

Wipe out is a surfing term that means "to fall off the board and get dumped in the water."

Devotion 26
Twisting the Facts

Gossiping is not a good idea. *Gossiping* is making up something about someone, talking behind his or her back, or twisting the facts in order to make a story more exciting. One of the things that I find awkward about being famous is that everybody wants to know everything about me. And when I choose not to tell them, they make things up.

There are lots of times that my friends and I could gossip if we wanted to. But we try hard not to gossip. The Bible says, "A gossip separates close friends" (Proverbs 16:28), and "A gossip betrays a confidence" (Proverbs 11:13). Sometimes it's hard to know exactly when news about somebody is just that—news or information—and not gossip.

Sharing news about others is fine—as long as it's done in a kind way. If you care about your friend, don't talk about his or her problems behind his or her back. Pray for your friend. I know

I don't like it when I hear untrue things going around about me. Nobody does. So be kind. Tell only the truth about other people—even if they're not your friends. If you don't know what's going on, don't make things up.

God's Words Inspire

A gossip betrays a confidence; so avoid a man who talks too much.
—Proverbs 20:19

Chatting with God

Jesus, I don't want to be a gossip. Forgive me for the times I have talked about someone behind his or her back. Help me to know when to share news about my friends and when to just keep quiet. In Jesus' name, amen.

Did You Know?

The Waimea Canyon on the island of Kauai is sometimes called the Grand Canyon of the Pacific.

Devotion 27
Doing the Impossible

Have you ever done something that you thought was completely impossible? Maybe you thought for sure you couldn't ride your bike or get on a horse. Maybe you were sure you would die before you got up in front of the class and recited a poem or jumped off the high dive. We've all had to face impossible moments in our lives. Most people thought it would be impossible for me to get back up on my surfboard after the attack—including me! We all struggled with the thoughts that I would be too scared to go in the water, that I wouldn't be able to duck dive under waves, or that I couldn't balance well enough to get up. But what a surprise I gave everyone! I was determined to do what others thought was impossible. But those things were not impossible in God's eyes, and that's why I was able to have that determination.

If you have accomplished just one thing that you originally thought was impossible, then you've seen what God can do. Now all you need to do is to trust him on the next impossible task that comes your way. Remember, "All things are possible with God" (Mark 10:27).

God's Words Inspire

With your help I can advance against a troop; with my God I can scale a wall.
                    —Psalm 18:29

Chatting with God

Almighty God, thank you for making everything possible. Give me courage to face the things that seem so impossible for me to handle. Encourage me with your love and your presence. Let me realize that by working with you, everything becomes possible. In Jesus' name, amen.

Did You Know?

Duck dive is a surfing term used to describe the way a surfer dives with the surfboard under a wave.

Devotion 28
I Believe

I believe in God. I believe that Jesus Christ
came to earth to save me from the result of
my sin. I believe that God is personal, loving,
and just. I have believed this for a very long
time. I guess I was about five years old when I
first recognized that God was real. And nobody
forced me to believe it. I just did.

Putting your faith in God is something you come
to on your own. Sure, parents and teachers can help
you. They can help you understand what Jesus and
the Bible are all about. But believing has to come
from your heart—it's a one-on-one thing.

My family is proud of their faith in God. My mom
is a real champion of prayer. Like the Bible says,
"Pray continually" (1 Thessalonians 5:17)—that's
my mom. But believing goes beyond reading the
Bible, praying, and going to church. Believing
starts deep in your heart and grows out from
there into everything you do and say.

Believing in God gives me a lot of
strength. I feel that my life is strong and
secure because it is based on God.
He is the foundation of my life.

God's Words Inspire

Believe in the Lord Jesus, and you will be saved.

—Acts 16:31

Chatting with God

Dear God, I believe that you are almighty. Thank you for sending Jesus to earth to save me from my sins. Help me to grow stronger in my faith in you so I can tell others about your love. In Jesus' name, amen.

Did You Know?

Some of my favorite Bible stories are Noah's ark (Genesis 6–9), Jonah and the whale (Jonah 1–2), and Jesus walking on the water (Matthew 14:22–32).

Devotion 29
Mirror Images

When I look in the mirror now, do you know what I see? I see me just as I am, with one arm. But I see that me as the normal me, and I'm okay with it. I don't see a handicapped person. I don't see what I don't have. I see what I am. And it's a good thing.

I do remember how I first reacted. A few days after the surgery, I looked in the mirror at myself. And my first thought was, "Oh my gosh, I have only one arm!" It was weird. There I was with one full arm on one side and this short, gauze-covered hunk of a shoulder on the other. But that was a long time ago, and I've gotten used to me this way.

Everyone thinks they have some kind of "handicap," even if it's not physical. Maybe you worry that you're too short, not good at sports, slow in math, or not rich enough. But you know what? That's all in your head. You *can* overcome a challenge without letting it become a handicap. Of course you can't do this alone—you need God's help. But if you work at it and have God on your side, you can do anything.

God's Words Inspire

Know that the LORD is God. It is he who made us, and we are his; we are his people, the sheep of his pasture.

—Psalm 100:3

Chatting with God

Dear Lord, I know that you made me in your image. I thank you for loving me just the way I am. Help me to accept what I can't change. Help me to work on the things that I can change. In Jesus' name, amen.

Did You Know?

"Stumpy" is the nickname that I use to refer to my left arm (or what's left of it).

Devotion 30

Outpouring of Aloha

In Hawaii the word *aloha* means a lot more than just *hello* and *good-bye*. It also means *love*. Hawaii is called The Aloha State. Hawaiians show aloha to one another. Things can be done in the spirit of aloha. Literally translated, *aloha* means "breath of God be upon you." It's kind of like saying, "May God bless you." It means you do something kind without expecting something in return.

When I came home from the hospital after the attack, my family and I were amazed at how people were willing to help: they brought food, cleaned the house, and eagerly started raising money to help pay expenses. And they were praying for us. Everybody wanted to help. Everybody wanted to show aloha.

There are lots of ways for us to show God's aloha (love) to others. We can pray for others. We can send notes to cheer them up. We can bring a meal or a special treat to someone who is sick. We can clean someone's house or do yard work. Showing aloha to our neighbors is what Jesus taught us to do.

God's Words Inspire

Serve one another in love. The entire law is summed up in a single command: "Love your neighbor as yourself."
— Galatians 5:13–14

Chatting with God

Dear God, thank you for loving us. Help us to love others out of a pure love, not with the purpose of getting something in return. Show us how we can love our neighbors in all kinds of ways that will be helpful to them and that will show your love. In Jesus' name, amen.

Did You Know?

Aloha can mean all of these things: hello, good-bye, love, mercy, compassion, grace, pity, greeting, loved one, to love, and to greet. Aloha!

Devotion 31
Lasting Happiness

Many people think clothes, fast cars, and popularity will make them happy. They think that the coolest bathing suit and a perfect body will make them happy. Or they think that the hottest surfboard will make them happy. Or they think they'll be happy if they're popular. Well, those kinds of things just won't bring lasting happiness.

The happiness we get from these things is temporary. Bathing suits and clothes wear out or go out of style. A surfboard gets dinged up or broken by a reef. Cars get rusty and old—just like my family's surf mobile.

But that doesn't mean we can't find happiness. Lasting happiness can be found in God's love. God's love and peace can bring us happiness even when we're in the worst situations. We also find joy in our loving relationships with friends and family. Think about a fun time you had. You can probably remember who you were with but not what you (or anyone else) was wearing. Stuff will rust or fade or break, but God's love will last forever.

God's Words Inspire

Do not store up for yourselves treasures on earth, where moth and rust destroy, and where thieves break in and steal. But store up for yourselves treasures in heaven, where moth and rust do not destroy, and where thieves do not break in and steal. For where your treasure is, there your heart will be also.
                    —Matthew 6:19–21

Chatting with God

Dear God, I have so many things. But what really makes me happy is knowing that your love for me will never change. Thank you for offering me what will bring me true happiness. In Jesus' name, amen.

Did You Know?

The 'i'iwi is a little red bird that is native to the island of Kauai. It is most commonly seen in the rain forest near the Alakai Swamp.

Devotion 32
God, Tired? Not!

After a long morning of surfing with my friends, my arm is like a noodle. Sometimes after being out all day, my arm gets so weak I just can't paddle out to the lineup anymore. When that happens, I know I need to take a break from surfing.

It's usually easy for my friends and me to find something else to do. We like to rest in the sand, eat, and talk while we watch the surf. We also like to walk along the beach and collect pretty shells. Sometimes we're even glad to head home and sit and hang out. Okay, that doesn't happen that often, but the change of pace can be refreshing and restful.

We all get tired. We all need to rest. We all need to get a good night's sleep at the end of the day (even if we haven't been surfing). And you know what comforts me? Knowing that God never gets tired of us or needs a break from his job. The Bible tells us very clearly that God "will neither slumber nor sleep" (Psalm 121:4).

God never needs a break. He never takes a nap. He's awake and with us 24/7. What a comfort! What a faithful God we have!

God's Words Inspire

Do you not know? Have you not heard? The LORD is the everlasting God, the Creator of the ends of the earth. He will not grow tired or weary, and his understanding no one can fathom. He gives strength to the weary and increases the power of the weak. Even youths grow tired and weary, and young men stumble and fall; but those who hope in the LORD will renew their strength. They will soar on wings like eagles; they will run and not grow weary, they will walk and not be faint.

—Isaiah 40:28–31

Chatting with God

Oh God, thank you for never falling asleep. Thank you for watching over me and for guiding me in the morning, through the afternoon, and all through the night. Help me to have restful sleep and wake up strong for a new day. In Jesus' name, amen.

Did You Know?

Noodles is a surfing term for how your arms feel after hours of intense surfing.

Devotion 33
Service Center

Ever since the attack, I have had some
new challenges—one being tying my
shoes. It is possible to do that with one hand,
but it's just too much of a bother most of the
time. Thank goodness I live in a warm climate
so I don't need to wear shoes with laces that
often. My choice of footwear is slippers, or—as
we pronounce them in Hawaii—"slippas." They're
practical, comfortable, and go with just about everything—especially bathing suits, which I wear pretty
much every day.

Hardly anyone who lives in Hawaii wears shoes
all the time. In fact, Hawaiians never wear shoes
in the house—they're all out on the front porch.
Taking your shoes off before going into the house
is a long-established Hawaiian custom. It could
be due to the red dirt that stains, or maybe it
reflects the Japanese culture.

In Jesus' day, people wore sandals and
always had dusty feet. So the custom was
to have a servant wash your feet when
you came into the house. Once when
Jesus was with his disciples, *he*

insisted on washing his disciples' feet to show them that everybody is equal in Christ and that we should gladly serve one another. Being humble and being willing to serve others is what loving Christ is all about.

God's Words Inspire

Now that I, your Lord and Teacher, have washed your feet, you also should wash one another's feet. I have set you an example that you should do as I have done for you. I tell you the truth, no servant is greater than his master, nor is a messenger greater than the one who sent him.

—John 13:14–16

Chatting with God

Dear Lord, help us to be humble. Let us remember the example of Christ acting as a servant. Make us willing to serve others as Christ did. In Jesus' name, amen.

Did You Know?

Slippas are sandals, more commonly known on the mainland as "flip-flops."

Devotion 34
What a Thrill!

Surfing is a thrilling experience for me.
Other people may get a rush out of playing basketball, writing a poem, or playing an
instrument. We get a thrill and a rush when
we use our talents to the ultimate. I get a rush
from dropping down the face of a wave, racing
down the line, and pulling a big snap off the lip.
For me, surfing is a good kind of addiction—a
pleasure that's hard to describe to anyone who has
not experienced it. It has grabbed me and won't let
me go. Every day I'm eager to get up and go surfing.
For a lot of people in the surfing world, surfing
is more than a rush or an exhilarating experience,
it's their god. They worship surfing and everything
that goes with it. Surfing is a big part of my life,
but being tight with God is more important to me
than surfing.
God gives us lots of things to enjoy in life.
No matter what our talent is, we need to realize that it is a gift from God. We can't do
anything on our own. God has given us
the ability to do what brings us such a
wonderful thrill and such great joy.
God wants us to enjoy the things

he's given us. "Delight yourself in the Lord and he will give you the desires of your heart" (Psalm 37:4).

God's Words Inspire

Jesus replied: " 'Love the Lord your God with all your heart and with all your soul and with all your mind.' This is the first and greatest commandment."
—Matthew 22:37 – 38

Chatting with God

Father God, thank you for all you have given me. Thank you for giving me unique abilities and experiences that bring excitement to my life and allow me to bring glory to your name. Help me to continue to enjoy those experiences but not to live for them. Help me to live for you alone. In Jesus' name, amen.

Did You Know?

The northwest side of the island of Kauai (where I live) is called the Na Pali Coast. The coastline is made up of two thousand-foot-high sea cliffs, and the only access to that whole twenty-two-mile stretch of land is by boat or foot. You can't drive there because there isn't a road that crosses those mountains and canyons.

Devotion 35
For **This I'm Thankful**

Every day I am in awe of the beauty of
Hawaii. I've lived in the same place all my life,
and I still find it so wonderful to live here. It is
unbelievably beautiful. Millions of tourists come
to Hawaii every year to experience some of the
great natural things about these islands. And I get
the privilege of living here!

When my mom and I head to the beach before
dawn, I often stick my head out the car window to
smell the tropical island scents: the salt air, the fra-
grance of the plumeria and pikake flowers, and the
wet foliage of the rain forest after a night of rain.

I love to hear the sound of the surf pounding
on the reef at night as I go to sleep—the louder
the better, 'cause that means the surf is up and
I'll be able to surf the next morning.

You can praise God for his wonderful
creation no matter where you live. What a
variety of places God has created! You
can praise him for the colors of fall,
for the snow of the winter, for the

mountains filled with snow for snowboarding, and for the endless plains that grow food. Nature shows off God's creation. Praise him for it.

God's Words Inspire

Praise the LORD from the earth, you great sea creatures and all ocean depths, lightning and hail, snow and clouds, stormy winds that do his bidding, you mountains and all hills, fruit trees and all cedars, wild animals and all cattle, small creatures and flying birds… Let them praise the name of the LORD, for his name alone is exalted; his splendor is above the earth and the heavens.

—Psalm 148:7–10, 13

Chatting with God

Oh wonderful Creator, I thank you for your great creation, for trees and seasons, for gentle breezes and howling winds, for lakes and seas, for deserts and farmland. All your creation shows your greatness; I praise you for it. In Jesus' name, amen.

Did You Know?

The Moanaowaiopuna Falls are the long, narrow waterfalls on the island of Kauai that became famous through the movie *Jurassic Park*.

Devotion 36
Our Own Personal Cheerleader

Everybody likes to cheer. We like to help a friend with a word of good cheer. Or we cheer each other up when we're feeling down. The Bible tells us that "a cheerful look brings joy to the heart" (Proverbs 15:30). We have cheerleaders at our basketball and football games. Our parents and friends cheer us on whether we compete in a spelling bee, or a piano recital, or a sports event. Cheerleading on the high school and college level has become a major sport with full TV coverage of the competitions. Cheerleading has even gone professional.

There is someone else who cheers for us. There is someone who is watching our every move and encouraging us to do a good job. When our family and friends have stopped cheering or don't show up, we all still have our own personal cheerleader who keeps on cheering for us. Can you guess? It's God. He is your personal cheerleader.

I picture God standing on the beach, or in the bleachers, or on the sidelines, cheering us on, celebrating our successes with shouts of joy. He's excited for us, saying, "Yeah, you go. You can do it! Great job!" He is with us wherever we go. He loves us and cheers us on through each day of our lives.

God's Words Inspire

For great is his love toward us, and the faithfulness of the Lord endures forever.
>   —Psalm 117:2

Chatting with God

Dear Lord, thank you for your great love for me. Thank you for being with me wherever I go and standing beside me in whatever I do. Thank you for being my personal cheerleader and for cheering me on even when I fall or mess up. In Jesus' name, amen.

Did You Know?

A *lei* is a wreath of fresh flowers, shells, or seeds usually worn around the neck, head, wrist, or ankle. It's a symbol of *aloha*, or welcome and love in Hawaii. Those funny little plastic and cloth ones you see in party stores don't even come close to the beauty of the real thing.

Devotion 37
We've Got Trouble

No matter how wonderful our life is, there will always be some kind of trouble that shows up. Sometimes we have small troubles: we catch the flu, we can't get our locker open, we miss the bus, or we have a fight with a friend. Sometimes there are troubles with a capital T: a tornado races through our town, a fire destroys our home, our parents divorce, or we're in a car accident. When I was little, Hurricane Iniki hit Kauai and devastated the island. That was a really hard time for my family. But we trusted the Lord, and God provided everything we needed.

I get letters all the time from people who want to share their troubles with me. They are hoping I will inspire them to keep going in order to get through a bad time. I've had troubles too, but God has helped me to move on.

Jesus warned us that life would be full of trouble. Troubles are pretty much unpredictable, but we can be encouraged that God is stronger and mightier than any trouble we face. In fact, he has already overcome it. No matter what happens, he's still in control. He will be with us to help us conquer any kind of trouble that comes our way.

God's Words Inspire

The LORD is good, a refuge in times of trouble. He cares for those who trust in him.
—Nahum 1:7

Chatting with God

Dear Lord, thank you for being with us in tough times. It is such a comfort to know you are stronger than any troubles we may have, big or small. Help us to put our trust in you. In Jesus' name, amen.

Did You Know?

In 1992, Hurricane Iniki caused approximately one billion dollars in damage. Most of the damage was on Kauai because Iniki passed directly over the island.

Devotion 38

Dream a Little Dream

Dreams can be very interesting; they seem to tell us what is on our minds. Sometimes we wake up knowing we had a good dream (even if we can't quite remember it). Other times we wake up in the middle of the night, frightened by a nightmare.

There are a lot of stories in the Bible about dreams. Joseph had some wild dreams about his brothers (Genesis 37); God spoke to King Solomon in a dream (1 Kings 3); and Daniel was able to explain King Nebuchadnezzar's wild dreams (Daniel 2). God spoke to people through dreams back then, and he does now too.

I usually have good dreams about surfing, about riding a wave of perfection. And for some reason, I always have two arms in my dreams. At other times my dreams fall in that nightmare category. I have had dreams about shadowy figures in the water or a shark heading for me or attacking me. I suppose that someday I'll no longer have those scary dreams about the past. I'd much rather dream about my future. I'd much rather look forward to the exciting things that God has in store for me.

God's Words Inspire

I will lie down and sleep in peace, for you alone, O LORD, make me dwell in safety.
    —Psalm 4:8

Chatting with God

Dear God, please bless me each night when I go to sleep. Give me dreams that are pleasant and sweet. Comfort me if I have bad dreams. Help me trust that you have good things planned for me. In Jesus' name, amen.

Did You Know?

Many surfers dream about riding the perfect wave. In their dreams the wave might be ten feet, or sixty feet, or one hundred feet high. Wow! Would that last one be a dream or a nightmare?

Devotion 39
Getting an *A* for Attitude

My family knows that I can be a bit grumpy and have a bad attitude from time to time. But having a bad attitude just drags you down and makes everyone around you miserable too. Now, of course, no one is giggly or in a good mood all the time. I've had major crying sessions—long ones—but they didn't last forever. And besides, I usually have my worst moments when nobody's around, like when I'm hiding out in my bedroom.

I've gotten a ton of emails and letters saying that I'm such an inspiration to people—that my attitude is so positive considering everything that's happened. Each time I hear that, I'm kind of amazed. I'm just a normal person. I'm nothing special. I guess I just try to be pleasant even when I'm not in a good mood.

When I have bad days and am giving my parents or brothers attitude, I try to remember how Jesus would have me act toward them. No matter what we're feeling inside, Jesus calls us to be selfless. We should ask Jesus to send the Holy Spirit to renew our thoughts and attitude and help us control our words and actions.

God's Words Inspire

There must be a spiritual renewal of your thoughts and attitudes. You must display a new nature because you are a new person, created in God's likeness—righteous, holy, and true.
—Ephesians 4:23–24 (NLT)

Chatting with God

Dear Lord, thank you for being part of my life. Let your Spirit renew me so that I have a good attitude. Let me be able to show others that I love you and that you live in me through everything I do and say. In Jesus' name, amen.

Did You Know?

The Hawaiian people are famous for their good attitude. They are extremely pleasant and friendly. That's why Hawaii is nicknamed The *Aloha* State.

Devotion 40
Raindrops Keep Falling

It rains a lot on Kauai. But Hawaii needs a
lot of rain to keep its tropical lush and green
look. Hawaii is in the tropics, and the tropics just
naturally get a lot of rain. Pretty much every day
it is raining somewhere on the island. Sometimes
we have rainstorms that last for days and weeks.
I really don't like it when it rains, because it limits
my surfing time. At least it doesn't get freezing cold
here when it rains. It's still warm enough to do fun
things outside with my friends.

One of the things we like to do during a storm is
surf on the wet grass. It's actually more like tobog-
ganing Hawaiian style because we sit down. We
find a very wet, steep, grassy hill and slide down
it on our body boards. It's a little bit crazy but a
lot of fun. And it sure is better than spending
all my time inside doing homework.

Although I'm not crazy about days
and days of rain, I know the rain is a gift
that God sends. Every place on earth
needs rain. And people who live

in countries that have no rain for years at a time suffer terribly. So the next time it rains, let's try to be thankful, even if it stops us from doing what we really want to do that day.

God's Words Inspire

Sing to the LORD with thanksgiving; make music to our God on the harp. He covers the sky with clouds; he supplies the earth with rain and makes grass grow on the hills.
—Psalm 147:7–8

Chatting with God

Dear heavenly Father, thank you for rain that refreshes the earth and supplies us with water to drink. Help me to rejoice on a rainy day, even if I can't do exactly what I had planned. Remind me that rain is a gift from you. In Jesus' name, amen.

Did You Know?

The average rainfall on the island of Kauai is 486 inches per year. Mount Waialeale on Kauai is one of the wettest spots in the world.

Devotion 41
How Strong Is God?

Our God is awesome. He is stronger and mightier than anything he has created.

Now when I try to think of something powerful and strong, naturally I think of the ocean. Large swells form huge waves. And when big waves crest, curl, and crash, they are powerful and downright noisy. They sound like thunder.

Almost everybody has seen the ocean. At least you've seen it on TV news during major storms that hit the coast. Everybody knows what big crashing waves look and sound like. Those of us in the surfing world actually go after the big waves. Some surfers spend lots of time and money going all over the world to find waves that are bigger than any wave they have ever seen. They say that when a fifty-foot wave crashes, the force and the noise are unbelievable.

But our God is stronger and bigger and more powerful than any wave of any height or strength in the world. He created those waves and he is in control of them all. "You rule over the surging sea; when its waves mount up, you still them" (Psalm 89:9). If we serve a God that big and that strong, there certainly isn't anything that we should be worried about.

God's Words Inspire

The seas have lifted up, O LORD, the seas have lifted up their voice; the seas have lifted up their pounding waves. Mightier than the thunder of the great waters, mightier than the breakers of the sea—the LORD on high is mighty.
—Psalm 93:3–4

Chatting with God

Oh mighty and wonderful God, I praise you for the glimpse of your power that I see in your creation. I praise you for your might and power. I thank you for being my God. Help me to feel secure knowing that just like you are in control of even the most powerful waves in the ocean, you are in control of the big situations in life. In Jesus' name, amen.

Did You Know?

During a hurricane, waves can be as high as one hundred feet (about the size of a ten-story building). The largest wave that anyone has ever surfed was seventy feet high. Pete Cabrinha rode that wave on January 10, 2004, at Jaws (Peahi) off the North Shore of the island of Maui in Hawaii.

Devotion 42
Popularity Isn't All That

Everybody wants to belong. Everybody wants to feel popular at some point. Most people want to feel accepted; to feel like they have people's approval. I think it's great to know that you have a bunch of friends to hang with. Some girls want to be popular with the girls. Some girls want to be popular with the guys. Sometimes they will do anything to be popular. They'll even do something they know is wrong. Or they'll try something their parents wouldn't approve of. That's not right. It's better to find a friend who likes you for what you are. Being popular with the wrong people who make you dump your best friend or ditch out on God is wrong. Even as popular as I've become, I don't let anyone tell me that I can't talk about God when I have a chance. Dumping God is not an option. Dumping my family and friends isn't either.

My family and friends back home don't let all this popularity stuff go to my head. I know I can count on them and God for support and love even if I stop being popular with the world. Popularity begins at home. Be sure you never give that up.

God's Words Inspire

Love must be sincere. Hate what is evil; cling to what is good. Be devoted to one another in brotherly love. Honor one another above yourselves.
                                   —Romans 12:9–10

Chatting with God

Dear God, thank you for being my best friend. Thank you for the friends you have given me. Help me to be humble in all areas of my life and to never sacrifice my friends and family or my witness of you for the chance to be popular. In Jesus' name, amen.

Did You Know?

It can be frustrating being recognizable as "that girl who got attacked by a shark." Almost anywhere I go people recognize me, ask for my autograph, or want to have their picture taken with me. But I have to remind myself why God put me in this position—to show his love and tell his story. Most of the time it doesn't bother me though. And when I'm back at home, everybody treats me normally—which is not only nice, but keeps me in the right frame of mind.

Devotion 43
Shine On

God has a lot more to offer than the world can ever give. What God gives lasts. Stuff of the world doesn't. I'm still alive because of God and his plan for me. He saved my life from a shark, and he has saved me from eternal death. And now I want to tell others about that.

I'm not crazy about doing interviews or standing up on a stage to tell my story, but I hope my life is like a Jesus Christ lighthouse. With Jesus in my heart, my life can shine for him. I hope that if people listen to me through my books, interviews, or movie, they will be drawn to learn more about the truth of God. He is a real and personal God. It doesn't matter who you are or what you've done or not done. God loves you and wants you to know him personally … period.

You can shine for Jesus too. You have a story about what God has done in your life that you can share with others. What you do and what you say to just one person or a group of people may make such an impact that it changes their life and the lives of maybe countless others in the future. Let your light shine for Jesus.

God's Words Inspire

You are the light of the world. A city on a hill cannot be hidden. Neither do people light a lamp and put it under a bowl. Instead they put it on its stand, and it gives light to everyone in the house. In the same way, let your light shine before men that they may see your good deeds and praise your Father in heaven.
—Matthew 5:14–16

Chatting with God

Dear Father in heaven, thank you for loving me and sending Jesus to save me. Give me courage to let my light shine for you. Help me to know what to say, and what to do to help others come to know you. In Jesus' name, amen.

Did You Know?

The Kilauea Lighthouse, located on the north end of Kauai, was built in 1913. It sent its light ninety miles out to sea, and its beacon stayed lit until 1976.

Devotion 44
And You Are?

Have you ever asked yourself the question, Who Am I? If you have, what did you say? I guess the first things you think of are your name, age, hair and eye color, where you live, how tall you are ... you know, that ordinary kind of stuff. You might say you are the daughter, sister, or friend of someone. Then you would probably move on to something you do well—a piano player, a cheerleader, a good friend, or a great reader. All of that would be very true about who you are.

But it all misses the most important thing. Number one on your list should be, "I am a child of God." The Bible says some incredible things about who we are in Christ. "How great is the love the Father has lavished on us, that we should be called children of God! And that is what we are!" (1 John 3:1). "For you created my inmost being; you knit me together in my mother's womb" (Psalm 139:13). "Long, long ago he decided to adopt us into his family through Jesus Christ. (What pleasure he took in planning this!)" (Ephesians 1:3–6, THE MESSAGE).

A lot of people want to identify me as the one-armed surfer girl, born and raised in Hawaii, or a shark-attack survivor. I get really tired of those descriptions because I'm so much more than that. I am a child of God. I belong to him and am loved by him. I hope you know that too.

God's Words Inspire

This is what the LORD says ... "Fear not, for I have redeemed you; I have summoned you by name; you are mine."
—Isaiah 43:1

Chatting with God

Dear God, I thank you for naming me as your child and for calling me your own. It is so wonderful that you know my name and that you love me as if I was the only person in the world! In Jesus' name, amen.

Did You Know?

Kamaaina is a Hawaiian word used to describe a child of the land or a longtime resident of Hawaii. A *malihini* is a newcomer to Hawaii or a tourist.

Devotion 45
Take Time for God

In the last couple of years I've been trying hard to spend time each day with God. Every day I make time to read my Bible and talk to God about all the stuff that's going on in my life. I know I can share anything with him. By reading God's Word and spending time with him, I develop a much closer relationship to him.

The Bible says, "Come near to God and he will come near to you" (James 4:8). This is so true. God won't force himself on you. That time with God will give you focus and remind you what God is all about.

Having devotions with God doesn't have to be a big deal. You don't need a special place. All you need is your Bible or a book of devotions (like this one), and a little bit of quiet. Think of it like being with a friend. You can tell God anything you would tell your very best friend. God wants to share every part of your life with him. There's nothing that you can't ask God. He will listen no matter what.

If you don't already set aside time to be with God, I hope you start.

I'm glad I do. It helps me put things in my life in perspective and develop an even closer relationship with Jesus Christ.

God's Words Inspire

Your word is a lamp to my feet and a light for my path.
— Psalm 119:105

Chatting with God

Oh God, thank you for speaking to me when I read your Word. I want to fall more and more in love with you each day. Continue to nourish me with spiritual food so I can be prepared to defend your Word and fight away temptation and wickedness. In Jesus' name, amen.

Did You Know?

The word for "Bible" in Hawaiian is *Paipala*. *Paipala Hemolele* is Hawaiian for "Holy Bible."

Devotion 46
Why Me?

When things go wrong or something bad happens to you, do you often ask, *Why me?* One of the most common questions people ask me is, "Do you often ask God why this happened to you?" I suppose I did think of that question. But I sure don't dwell on it. God has his reasons.

I can now see that God is using me in a unique way to tell others about him. God is working in and through me. And it's pretty awesome to be a part of that.

There are lots of stories in the Bible about challenges people went through. One guy, named Job, had all kinds of bad things happen: his whole family died, he lost all his livestock and possessions, and then on top of that he got boils. He didn't have a clue why any of this stuff was happening to him. His wife told him to blame and curse God. But he wouldn't do it. In all Job's suffering and pain, he still praised God and trusted that God would heal him.

It's normal to wonder why, but you can trust that God has a plan and that he loves you. He will see you through anything.

God's Words Inspire

My salvation and my honor depend on God, he is my mighty rock, my refuge. Trust in him at all times, O people; pour out your hearts to him, for God is our refuge.
                    —Psalm 62:7–8

Chatting with God

Oh God, help me to believe that no matter what happens you will stay by my side and see me through anything. I put my trust in you, for there is nothing or no one mightier. In Jesus' name, amen.

Did You Know?

Surfers have to have exact timing and sharp reflexes to stay balanced. They also need to trust their instincts as to what a breaking wave will do.

Devotion 47
Teeming Millions

The first chapter of Genesis tells us about what God created. But not until you are up close to the tropical life that lives in the ocean do you get an idea of what God meant when he said, "Let the waters teem with living creatures" (Genesis 1:20).

When the surf is flat, my friends and I sometimes go snorkeling near the coral reef. When you step into the water and look through your mask, you just can't believe that there are that many fish swimming around right where you are. It is amazing! As often as we've done this, there is always something new to see. I am in awe of what God has created for us to enjoy. Don't you think he must have had a great time coming up with all those ideas for little sparkly fish? And there are loads of other creatures as well.

If you don't live near the tropics to enjoy snorkeling, visit an aquarium in a nearby city. That will give you an idea of how marvelous these "teeming" creatures are. What an amazing world God has made! What an amazing God we serve! Praise him!

God's Words Inspire

How many are your works, O LORD! In wisdom you made them all; the earth is full of your creatures. There is the sea, vast and spacious, teeming with creatures beyond number—living things both large and small.
—Psalm 104:24–25

Chatting with God

Almighty Creator, thank you for your wonderful creatures that fill the oceans. I praise you for the marvelous variety of tropical fish that you have put here for us to enjoy. Thank you for allowing us to experience this delight. In Jesus' name, amen.

Did You Know?

The Na Pali Coast of Kauai is a great area for snorkeling. The only way to reach some of the best areas for snorkeling is by boat.

Devotion 48
Lots of Little Presents

Have you ever given someone a gift and then found out they never used it? That hurts. Well, God gives us gifts. Some gifts we have already opened. We're using them right now and enjoying them. Other gifts we know are there, but we just haven't unwrapped them completely.

The kind of gifts I'm talking about don't come in cardboard boxes with bright paper and bows. These gifts are gifts of talent, opportunity, or personality—that kind of thing.

All of us have unique gifts. God gives different gifts to different people so that the world works together better. If we all were good at the same stuff, a lot of things would be left undone. Some of us have the gift of speaking. Some of us have the gift of making others laugh. You might have the gift of being a great friend or listener. Maybe you excel at math, writing, or science. Maybe you're great at babysitting or playing the piano or surfing (yeah!). Gifts come in all different varieties.

Accept your gifts gladly and use them to God's glory. Don't hide your talents or be embarrassed by them. God wants you to use your gifts today and to develop them to use them even better in the future.

God's Words Inspire

There are different kinds of gifts, but the same Spirit. There are different kinds of service, but the same Lord. There are different kinds of working, but the same God works all of them in all men.
—1 Corinthians 12:4–6

Chatting with God

Dear God, thank you for being generous. Thank you for giving me so many good gifts. Help me to discover them and use them now for your glory. In Jesus' name, amen.

Did You Know?

A skill a surfer needs to learn is how to do a turtle roll in rough, white water. This is when you roll over while hanging on to your surfboard so the breaking wave just rumbles over you and your board without sweeping you back toward the beach.

Devotion 49
Lots of Courage

It takes courage to face some of the ordinary things in life: the first day of going to a new school, trying to make a new friend, reading out loud, or wearing your hair different than before. It takes courage to do what you know is right or to follow what your parents say when that's not what everybody else is doing. It takes courage to stand up for your faith in God when others think it's silly and weak to rely on him. Having courage is doing something even though you're afraid.

Sometimes I need courage to go out in the ocean and surf. I get a funny feeling that creeps me out. But I know of ways to build my courage. My mom prays for my peace of mind when I'm in the water. She knows that if I can concentrate and stay calm, I can get in my zone and surf really well. Being with my friends out there also helps. We chat back and forth, or we all sing something. And I pray. Just remembering that God is always with me keeps me calm and courageous.

When you're afraid, pray for God to give you courage. He will help. So be strong and courageous. God is on your side. He can help you through anything.

God's Words Inspire

Be strong and courageous. Do not be afraid or terrified ... for the Lord your God goes with you; he will never leave you nor forsake you.
— Deuteronomy 31:6

Chatting with God

Dear God, thank you for promising to always be with me no matter where I go or what I do. Help me to be courageous to do what's right when I'm afraid of what other kids will think or when I'm not sure of myself. Give me the courage to keep going. In Jesus' name, amen.

Did You Know?

After the attack, the medical attendant in the ambulance whispered part of that verse into my ear: "The Lord will never leave you nor forsake you." I'll never forget that. And you know what? It's true!

Devotion 50
Don't Just Believe It ... Do It!

The easy parts of believing in God are reading the Bible, praying, and going to church. The hard part is putting what we believe into action. Every day we should be doing something that shows that we have faith in God. We can't hide in our closets and worship. Everywhere we go we should be acting out our faith.

We can do this in little ways. We can watch what we say by not talking trash or gossiping. We can be positive, honest, and kind (even when we're not happy).

We can demonstrate our faith in big ways too. My youth group goes on a mission trip to Mexico to help the people there. Since we don't speak much Spanish, our actions have to show we are doing this because of God's love. I sponsor a child in El Salvador through World Vision. By giving just a few dollars a month, I help this little girl get food, shelter, and an education.

You and your family can help people in your own community in many ways. You may donate clothes, books, toys, and food. You may volunteer your time: look in your local newspaper for a list of organizations that need help. You may give a portion of your allowance or babysitting money to a favorite charity. If you keep your eyes open, you will find many ways that you can put your faith in action.

God's Words Inspire

Do not merely listen to the word, and so deceive yourselves. Do what it says.
—James 1:22

Chatting with God

Oh God, I want to show your love to others. Open my eyes and show me what I can do each day to let others know that I love you. Let my faith in you shine as I put my faith into action. In Jesus' name, amen.

Did You Know?

There is a group of Christian surfers who have a magazine called *Christian Surf*. They covered the story about the fund-raiser held after my attack.

Devotion 51
Jesus Is My Every Day

Jesus is part of my everyday life. He's not just someone I think about and worship on Sunday. He's more than just someone I acknowledge in front of my church friends, my family, or an audience of Christians. Jesus is part of everything I do and say.

I try to talk about Jesus every chance I get. I'm not crazy about doing interviews, but if it gives me a chance to talk about Jesus, then I'll do it with the hope that somebody who hears about what God has done in my life will come to know Jesus.

I'm not the only one who has a chance to talk about Jesus. You do too. Every day you have a chance to talk about him to your friends. I know it's a scary thing to include Jesus in all this and to talk about him, but you can do it. Try telling others what Jesus has done for you. Tell them about the joy that Jesus brings to your life even when things aren't going great. Tell them how

God has answered your prayers. Use Jesus' name appropriately, not by swearing.

Don't just keep Jesus a Sunday thing or a family thing. Make Jesus part of your every day.

God's Words Inspire

Make the most of every opportunity. Let your conversation be always full of grace, seasoned with salt, so that you may know how to answer everyone.
—Colossians 4:5–6

Chatting with God

Oh Lord Jesus, thank you for being with me all the time. Let me praise and honor your name every day, in every way so that others know you are my all-time, everyday Jesus. In Jesus' name, amen.

Did You Know?

When a friend of mine got hurt in a surfing competition, a group of Christians I was with stopped everything and prayed for her right there on the beach.

Devotion 52
Don't Stress Out!

When my life gets stressed out and way too busy, I just want to run off and go surfing. Surfing calms me down and helps me focus. A lot of my time these days is spent traveling and making appearances on TV shows or at church services. This stuff is exciting, but it can get tiring and stressful. There are times that I just can't wait to do a bunch of normal stuff with my friends back home. You can probably relate.

A lot of people think it's silly that teenagers get stressed out. But we do. Homework, tests, projects, parents' expectations, doing what our coaches want, fitting in time with friends, and trying to find enough time to do the stuff we *really* want to do can leave us anxious and stressed. Too often there just aren't enough hours in any one day to fit all the stuff in.

The Bible tells us not to be stressed and anxious. We can go to God when we feel this way and dump it all on him. "Cast all your anxiety on God because he cares for you" (1 Peter 5:7).

What a great idea! Sometimes it's just not that easy to let go of it all and leave it up to God. But we have to try. Maybe if we practice with the little things, it will get easier for us to trust God with the big things.

God's Words Inspire

So do not fear, for I am with you; do not be dismayed, for I am your God. I will strengthen you and help you; I will uphold you with my righteous right hand ... For I am the LORD, your God, who takes hold of your right hand and says to you, ... do not fear; I will help you.
—Isaiah 41:10,13

Chatting with God

Dear Lord and Father, thank you for caring about me and all that I do. Help me to come to you when I am stressed and anxious. Help me to hand over all my worries to you, to let you work them out. In Jesus' name, amen.

Did You Know?

When I travel to different places around the world, I say that I am *off-island*.

Devotion 53
Running from God

Do you remember the Jonah story? He was the guy who ran away. When God told him to go preach in Nineveh, Jonah ran off in a boat in the opposite direction. He got into lots of trouble because he didn't want to do what God had called him to do—something hard and uncomfortable.

Sometimes I feel like I'm acting like Jonah. I'm not always comfortable with what God asks me to do. Sometimes he gives me a nudge to talk to a specific person, but I don't want to, and I come up with excuses. "What will she think of me?" "I don't have time." "I'll do it in a few minutes." Or, "I'll talk to her if she starts talking to me first."

God sometimes calls us to do what we're uncomfortable with. Obeying God the first time he asks is always best, even if what we are asked to do isn't what we want to do. God loves us, and he knows what's best for us. Running away from his call will only get you into trouble. We need to trust him and obey him as we follow where he leads.

God's Words Inspire

We know that we have come to know him if we obey his commands ... if anyone obeys his word, God's love is truly made complete in him. This is how we know we are in him: Whoever claims to live in him must walk as Jesus did.
—1 John 2:3, 5–6

Chatting with God

Dear God, next time you put something on my heart to do, I want to do it with no second thoughts. Help me to trust you. I want to obey you the first time you ask. Help me to listen to your voice and follow. In Jesus' name, amen.

Did You Know?

Kauai has 110 miles of coastline. It has more long, white, sandy beaches than any of the other Hawaiian islands.

Devotion 54
Looking at the Inside

Our friends and family who know us well see past the obvious things of our appearance. Once people get to know us well, they forget to see some of the surface stuff: like the fact that we have glasses, braces, big feet, or one arm. All they see is this great person.

God knows us well. He sees way beyond the surface stuff. It doesn't matter if we are the smartest in the class or the prettiest or wear the nicest clothes. God looks deep inside of us. He goes straight to the heart.

God cares if we are kind and loving, obedient and respectful, thoughtful and courteous, generous and compassionate. God looks at our motivations and knows our deepest secrets. He looks at who we really are.

We still need to take care of our bodies, but we shouldn't forget what's really important about ourselves and other people. It's not all the glam and the glitter; it's what's in your heart that counts.

God's Words Inspire

The LORD does not look at the things man looks at. Man looks at the outward appearance, but the LORD looks at the heart.

—1 Samuel 16:7

Chatting with God

Dear Jesus, thank you for seeing the real me. Help me to realize that what really counts and what you look at is what goes on in my heart. Help me to be more like you. Help me to see other people by what's in their hearts, not by what they look like. In Jesus' name, amen.

Did You Know?

One of the best things about being in my hometown is that my neighbors don't even notice that I have only one arm. They have all gotten used to me this way, and it's no big deal anymore.

Devotion 55
Oh, Yes You Can

When was the last time you said (or even thought), "I can't do that!"? What was it that you were sure you couldn't do: Ice skate? Do ten push-ups? Run a mile? Complete eight story problems in math? Tell your friend about Jesus? Try out for the school play? Pray out loud? Be nice to the person who is mean to you?

In the last couple of years I've done lots of things that I once would have said I couldn't do. I have: surfed with one arm; appeared on stage in front of thousands of people; met Oprah, Tony Hawk, Janet Jackson, Amy Smart, and other famous people; written a book; and traveled on mission trips around the world. (Well, you get the idea ... enough about me.)

Through all this I found out something. I don't have to do it all on my own. God is there to help me.

God may want to do big things in your life too. You can't expect to do them on your own. But with God anything is possible. With your willingness and his strength, the two of you can accomplish really cool things.

God's Words Inspire

I can do everything through him who gives me strength.
—Philippians 4:13

Chatting with God

Dear God, thank you for being strong when I am weak. Thank you for sharing your strength with me so that I can accomplish great things for you. Give me courage to try. Give me an open heart to trust you. In Jesus' name, amen.

Did You Know?

Explorer Captain James Cook stumbled on Kauai in 1778 while sailing from Tahiti toward North America. He was the first European to set foot in the Hawaiian Islands.

Devotion 56
The Best of Friends

All of us want to have good friends—those who like us for who we are and not for what we can do. We will have friends who come and go, but the very best kind of friend sticks with you no matter what happens. My very best friends are those I've had since *hanabata days*.

A good friend cheers you on, isn't jealous, accepts you for who you are; stays by your side when things go really wrong, and reminds you where you've come from. This is also a good check to see how *you* stand up to being a good friend to others.

Jesus is not only a good friend; he's the best! He never leaves us or forgets about us (Joshua 1:5). He made us the way we are and loves us just that way. He gave his life for us so that we could live. And he's waiting for us to join him in heaven someday.

I hope that everyone finds at least one really good, true friend to hang with. And I also hope that you come to find that Jesus is your very best friend of all, to hang with now … and forever.

God's Words Inspire

A friend loves at all times.
— Proverbs 17:17

Chatting with God

Dear Jesus, thank you for being my very best friend. Thank you for giving me the Bible that teaches me how to show love to others. Help me to be a good friend. Please bring me friends that will reflect you in their lifestyle and in their love for others. In Jesus' name, amen.

Did You Know?

Hanabata days is the Hawaiian way of referring to days of childhood. *Hanabata* means "nose butter," or "snotty nose."

Devotion 57
Being a Winner

Winning isn't as easy as it looks. If you've ever watched professional athletes do their thing, you know they make it look easy. Watching the Olympics last year made me think of that. All of those athletes were great at what they did, like skiing, snowboarding, and ice-skating. But I know that it takes a lot of perseverance (or stick-to-itiveness) to get to that level. Behind every winning athlete there are hours and hours and hours of practice, practice, and more practice. And there's not just the fun part of doing the sport. Every sport requires intense training: push-ups, sit-ups, running for miles, building muscles, building stamina, and working on technique. You can't just jump on a board and think you'll win the first contest. No, it takes discipline, hard work, keeping a good attitude when you wipe out, and perseverance.

All that we do in life requires perseverance: being a good friend, being a Christian, playing the violin, or writing a story. The more we practice doing these things, the better we become at them.

So hang in there, no matter what it is God is asking you to do. He wants you to be a winner.

God's Words Inspire

I know your deeds, your hard work and your perseverance.
—Revelation 2:2

Chatting with God

Dear God, thank you for my talents. Keep me strong to persevere and practice, practice, practice, so that I can bring glory to your name in whatever I do. In Jesus' name, amen.

Did You Know?

Formula for winning: perfect your skill + keep a positive attitude = a winner.

Devotion 58
Living Temples

Our bodies are God's temple. God's Spirit lives inside of us, so our bodies are holy places. We are his temple.

You've probably seen pictures of the great cathedrals of Europe. These are old churches built to honor God. When people enter Saint Peter's Basilica in Rome, they look with respect and act reverently. Even sightseers who don't even believe in God visit this holy place and treat it that way.

We need to treat our "temples," our bodies, with respect too. If God lives in us, then we need to take good care of his "house." This means exercise, eat healthy foods, and do those things that will make us healthy and not hurt our bodies. We also need to be aware of what we feed our minds. Don't watch trashy movies or TV shows. Instead, fill your mind with things that honor God.

We need to take good care of ourselves. We belong to God, and we need to take good care of his stuff.

God's Words Inspire

*Don't you know that you yourselves are
God's temple and that God's Spirit lives in you?*
—1 Corinthians 3:16

Chatting with God

Dear God, thank you for your Spirit that lives in me. Help me to respect my body as your temple. Make me strong to resist temptation. Give me strength to exercise regularly. Make me wise to feed my body right. In Jesus' name, amen.

Did You Know?

People were surfing in Hawaii even before Christopher Columbus sailed to the New World in 1492.

Devotion 59
Speak Up

If there's a great new product to buy—
toys, video games, books, or movies—we
hear about it. It's advertised on TV, on the
radio, in magazines, and in newspapers. If it's
impressive, soon everybody's talking about it
and wants one. Nobody keeps it a secret.

Well, you know what? Christians have the
greatest thing in the world to tell others about:
God's love. It should be natural to share the greatest
news in the world with our friends and others. God's
love is FREE—one hundred percent free: no waiting in lines, no big price tag, no limited quantities.
Everybody can afford it. They just have to know
about it and accept it.

It's our job to advertise this great free gift. And
yet many of us, including me, get shy and quiet
when it comes to sharing Jesus with others.

You are a walking and talking advertisement
for God. A pleasant attitude and a smile
will attract people, but you have to speak
out and tell them about it too. So open
up and, speak out, tell others about
God's love.

God's Words Inspire

Give thanks to the LORD, call on his name; make known among the nations what he has done, and proclaim that his name is exalted. Sing to the LORD, for he has done glorious things; let this be known to all the world.

—Isaiah 12:4–5

Chatting with God

Dear God, you have given the world the great gift of your love. I thank you and praise you for doing that. Make me strong to be able to advertise to the people of the world that you love them. In Jesus' name, amen.

Did You Know?

Hawaii is well advertised. Over six million people come to the Hawaiian Islands every year on vacation.

Devotion 60
It's a **Bummer**

Do you ever get discouraged? Are you
ever just plain down in the dumps? Do
you have days when you think you're a big
nothing? A failure? I get that way sometimes.
Especially if I didn't do my best while competing
in a surfing contest.

I guess all people get this way sometimes.
Even great people in the Bible felt this way. Moses
and Joshua, along with God's people, felt this way
many times while they waited to get into the land
God had promised them. But God never left their
side. He gave them words of encouragement when
they were discouraged.

God is there for you too. Sometimes his support comes through encouraging words from
friends or your family or a teacher or a coach.
When I'm all bummed out about doing something dumb, my dad always tells me, "Shake it
off, Bethany. Move on. Leave it behind you."
God doesn't want us to dwell on our
mess-ups. Focus on what is ahead and
learn from the past by turning it into
a tool for growth.

God's Words Inspire

If the LORD delights in a man's way, he makes his steps firm; though he stumble, he will not fall, for the LORD upholds him with his hand.
        —Psalm 37:23–24

Chatting with God

Dear Jesus, stay close to me when I'm discouraged. Whisper in my ear that you are by my side. Remind me to cheer up and be strong. In Jesus' name, amen.

Did You Know?

The Na Pali Coast on Kauai has twenty-two miles of scenic coastline. It's Hawaii's most remote wilderness area. You can only get there by air, by sea, or on foot.

Devotion 61
Sweet Sleeping

Sometimes I have a hard time falling asleep. My mind gets stuck in fast gear, and I just can't turn things off. You've probably had nights like that too. Maybe you're worried about what's going on in school. Or you're thinking about a problem with a friend. Maybe the dark makes any little noise seem huge and frightening.

At times when I can't stop thinking about all that's going on, you know what I do? I make my mind think about God instead. I think about how strong he is and that he controls the world. Reading God's Word just before I go to sleep can really help me relax and rest peacefully.

Isn't it amazing that God talks about sleep in the Bible? You would think that there would be lots more important stuff to talk about than sleep. Since God includes it, it must be important. Sleep is his gift to us because he loves us (Psalm 127:2). The Bible also promises, "When you lie down, you will not be afraid; when you lie down, your sleep will be sweet"

(Proverbs 3:24). That's a real nice thought to end any day.

God's Words Inspire

I will lie down and sleep in peace, for you alone, O LORD, make me dwell in safety.
—Psalm 4:8

Chatting with God

Dear heavenly Father, thank you for peaceful sleep. Thank you for watching over me both day and night so that I know I'm safe in your care. I pray that you will give me lots of rest tonight so I wake up refreshed and ready to start a new day. In Jesus' name, amen.

Did You Know?

Hawaii is in a separate time zone (Hawaiian Standard Time) from the rest of the United States. It's five hours behind what goes on in New York City. That means when people in New York are getting out of bed, we're still catching Zs here in Hawaii.

Devotion 62
Good to the Finish

We usually start a new project with big plans and lots of enthusiasm. Then somewhere along the way we get bored with what we're doing and quit. Maybe you've started a craft project, gotten half-finished, and then shoved it in the back of your closet. Maybe you've joined a sports team or started music lessons and given up on it after only a few months.

These things take perseverance. You have to push through the hard parts, the learning parts, to find the fun again. That's what it's like with surfing. There are some days when you're just struggling to catch waves or your balance is off and you keep falling. Or you get hurt, and it scares you to go back out. It's these times that require determination and perseverance. If you want to keep progressing, you have to keep practicing. It is the same in our walk with God. To keep moving forward and growing, you have to keep doing—even if you have no motivation or everything is going wrong. Do what you set out to do. Most worthwhile things require effort and commitment to finish. Don't quit in the middle. If you are overwhelmed, then set shorter goals to reach the big one.

God's Words Inspire

The best thing you can do right now is to finish what you started last year and not let those good intentions grow stale. Your heart's been in the right place all along. You've got what it takes to finish it up, so go to it. Once the commitment is clear, you do what you can, not what you can't.
—2 Corinthians 8:10–11
(The Message)

Chatting with God

Dear Jesus, forgive me for not always finishing what I plan on doing. Help me to stay focused. Help me to get through the tough parts of learning to master a skill. Thank you for promising to be by my side all the way through the finish. In Jesus' name, amen.

Did You Know?

In 2005 I won my first professional surfing contest! It was the O'Neill Island Girl Junior Pro. It was a great feeling to accomplish that goal.

Devotion 63
Something to Brag About

From time to time everyone wants to brag about something. Well, you know what? Christians have something to brag about, big time. Our God! Our God is just awesome! He is more powerful and mighty than anything we can think of or know about. He understands us and knows every thought we have—even when we don't understand our own thoughts. That blows my mind!

God is so great. He shows kindness, justice, and righteousness on earth absolutely perfectly every day. That means that he is right here in the middle of all that's going on in the world. He takes great pleasure in working justly and showering blessings of kindness on his children every day. He likes doing it so much that he delights in it.

The Bible tells us that we should boast in God all day long (Psalm 44:8), for he is a wonderful and awesome God!

I'm so proud to be a follower of the almighty God, the Creator of the

universe who is alive and works his wonders and justice in the world and in my life every day.

God's Words Inspire

*"Let him who boasts boast about this: that he
understands and knows me, that I am the LORD, who
exercises kindness, justice and righteousness on earth,
for in these I delight," declares the LORD.*
                              —Jeremiah 9:24

Chatting with God

Lord Jesus, forgive me for anytime I have
ever bragged about myself. Help me to boast
about your kindness and justice rather than
myself or my accomplishments. Fill me with
your love. In Jesus' name, amen.

Did You Know?

Hawaii has mild temperatures all year
round, ranging from seventy to eighty
degrees!

Devotion 64
The Problem Fixer

Everybody has problems that they wish would go away. Like your best friend isn't speaking to you (and you don't know why); or your parents are arguing again and it scares you; or you're frightened to ride the bus because the big kids in the back are always acting up. Some problems seem as huge as a mountain. Don't you just hate it when there's nothing you can do to fix a problem?

Well, you know what? There is something you can do. You can pray. And you can have faith that God will handle the problem. Jesus told his disciples this long ago. The disciples were asked to heal a boy, but they couldn't do it. So Jesus healed the boy. Then he told the disciples that if they had enough faith, even as small as a mustard seed, they could do this (Matthew 17:14–21).

Remember, no problem is too big for God. He can handle anything. You just have to ask him to help and believe that he will.

God's Words Inspire

Jesus replied, "I tell you the truth, if you have faith and do not doubt, . . . you can say to this mountain, 'Go, throw yourself into the sea,' and it will be done. If you believe, you will receive whatever you ask for in prayer."
—Matthew 21:21–22

Chatting with God

Dear Jesus, please help me to run to you when I face problems that scare me or that I can't fix on my own. I believe that you can do anything. Nothing is impossible for you. Thank you for being almighty. In Jesus' name, amen.

Did You Know?

Ho'olu is the Hawaiian word for "please." *Mahalo* is the Hawaiian word for "thank you."

Devotion 65

Brain Food: No Junk Allowed

Everybody knows you have to snack on the right kind of foods to have a healthy body. That's also true for the food we feed our brains. What we think about, what we read, and what we see on TV, in the movies, or on the Internet is all brain food.

Just as you can choose what kinds of food go into your mouth, you can also choose the kinds of stuff that go into your brain. Your parents or teachers can help you choose wisely. With TV shows, decide at the beginning of the week what shows you want to watch. Then only turn on the TV when those shows are coming on. Don't sit mindlessly watching any old thing. Carefully select the movies you watch. Check out the rating and read the reviews ahead of time. And when you're online, be careful to stay on parent-approved sites.

God's Word will make you strong. Read the Bible every day. It's super food for your mind and soul. Spend time in church praising God. Singing and worshiping are also health foods for your mind and soul. Feed your mind the good stuff. It will make you healthy.

God's Words Inspire

Finally, brothers, whatever is true, whatever is noble, whatever is right, whatever is pure, whatever is lovely, whatever is admirable—if anything is excellent or praiseworthy—think about such things. Whatever you have learned or received or heard from me, or seen in me—put it into practice. And the God of peace will be with you.
—Philippians 4:8–9

Chatting with God

Dear God, forgive me for not always choosing right. Help me to select good food for my mind. Help me to avoid the junk that is all around me and is so easy to stuff my brain with. Make me want to think right and pure thoughts. In Jesus' name, amen.

Did You Know?

Kauai is a pretty simple place. We have no ice-skating rinks, no miniature golf, no go-cart place, one bowling alley, only one major road that circles the island, and two movie theaters. But Hawaii altogether has more famous surfing spots per mile than any place else in the world!

Devotion 66
The Guilt Dumpster

It's a natural thing to feel guilty when we do something we know is wrong. Guilt hangs on you like a backpack full of books. And the longer you carry it around, the heavier it gets. It just drags you down. It makes you think about the past, not look ahead to the future.

You may be able to hide your guilt from others, but you can't hide your guilt from God. He knows everything. The Bible says, "You know my folly, O God; my guilt is not hidden from you" (Psalm 69:5). But the good news is that he provides us with a guilt dumpster. We can come to him, tell him all about it, and throw away our guilt. We don't have to carry it around forever. We can start focusing on our hope for the future.

And what's better yet is that when we dump our guilt on God, he forgives us our sins (Psalm 103:3); and then makes us clean again—"whiter than snow" (Psalm 51:7). What a great deal.

So don't drag around your old guilt. Don't try hiding it someplace. Get it out. Tell it to God and throw it in God's guilt dumpster. He will listen and forgive.

God's Words Inspire

Finally, I confessed all my sins to you and stopped trying to hide them. I said to myself, "I will confess my rebellion to the LORD." And you forgave me! All my guilt is gone.
— Psalm 32:5 (NLT)

Chatting with God

Dear God, I know I am guilty of doing and saying and thinking wrong things. Help me to unload my guilt by handing it over to you. Please forgive me and make me clean again so I can live joyfully. In Jesus' name, amen.

Did You Know?

There are places on Kauai where the trash truck doesn't come to pick up the trash. The people who live there have to take their rubbish to the dump so it doesn't stink up and pollute their homes. (It reminds me of how we need to take our guilt to God's dumpster so it doesn't stink up and pollute our lives.)

Devotion 67
Laugh a Lot

Have you ever just looked at your best
friend and started laughing? Sometimes
all it takes is a look between friends and the
giggles begin. It feels so good to let go and
laugh till your stomach hurts.

I love laughing. Laughter makes everything
brighter. Laughter is sunshine. It makes you feel
warm inside. The more you share laughter, the better it is. Laughing with your friends is one of the best
experiences in the world.

Laughter is a sign that the joy of Jesus fills our
lives and makes us happy. We laugh because God
has given us so many wonderful things in life to be
happy about: family and friends, pets, sunshine,
surfing (yeah!), and a ka-zillion other things.

God created laughter. He wants us to be
happy. He wants our lives to be filled with
so much joy that we bubble up with laughter and let it come out. Even giggles are
good things. Our God is not a miserable,
grouchy God. He is a God of joy and
laughter. This is part of God's gift of
joy to us.

God's Words Inspire

Our mouths were filled with laughter, our tongues with songs of joy. Then it was said among the nations, "The LORD has done great things for them." The LORD has done great things for us, and we are filled with joy.
— Psalm 126:2–3

Chatting with God

Dear Jesus, thank you for the gift of laughter. Thank you for filling my life with joy. Please fill my every day with laughter with friends and family. Let others see that my joy and laughter comes from you. In Jesus' name, amen.

Did You Know?

The Hawaiian language does not have words for north, south, east, and west. They indicate directions with phrases: *makai* means "toward the sea" and *mauka* means "inland, or toward the mountains."

Devotion 68
The Body Machine

Our bodies are made of an amazing combination of systems that work together seamlessly: muscles, bones, nerves, and more. God thought all of this up when he created us. This physical machine called a body keeps going and going and going.

It's amazing how many things we do automatically. When I go surfing, my body knows exactly what to do. I don't have to think about each specific move. Surfing involves every one of my senses too. My eyes select the best waves to ride and help me identify the direction of the current. When the breeze touches my wet skin, I can tell the wind direction. My ears help me hear what's going on around me. I can smell the salty ocean air, and I usually get a good taste of the salt water. I don't have to actually think about any of these things; they just happen automatically.

God made a very beautiful thing when he made our bodies. The Bible says that he "knit me together in my mother's womb" (Psalm 139:13). He has known us since before we were born.

That's so cool. What a wonderful creation
we are!

God's Words Inspire

*I praise you because I am fearfully and wonderfully
made; your works are wonderful, I know that full well.*
—Psalm 139:14

Chatting with God

Dear God, thank you for creating my body that
is so wonderful. Thank you for the health and the
strength you give me each day. Help me to take
good care of your masterpiece. In Jesus' name,
amen.

Did You Know?

Wind direction is commonly discussed among Hawaiian surfers because it can affect the surf conditions.
Trade winds blow predominately from the northeast.

Devotion 69
A Day to Rejoice

To get the most out of every day, I start my day very early. Most mornings my mom and I are up before anyone else in the family. Even on the days that are stormy or rainy, I'm out of bed and on my way to check the surfing conditions at the beach. But I like days best when the morning is clear, and the sunrise promises to be warm and bright. On a really great day, when the weather is just right and the surf is firing, I can surf all morning and all afternoon. But every new day brings its own excitement.

Every day is a day to rejoice and be glad. Why? Because God loves us. The Bible says we should ask God to "satisfy us in the morning with your unfailing love, that we may sing for joy and be glad all our days" (Psalm 90:14). That means we can find joy every day, not just on some days: like the last day of school, the beginning of a long weekend, your birthday, or (for me) the perfect surfing day. There is something in each day that we can be happy about! Just knowing

God has paid for all our sins is plenty of reason to be happy!

Every day is a day that God has made. A new day is God's gift to us to use the best way we can. Let's rejoice for every new morning.

God's Words Inspire

This is the day that the LORD has made; let us re-joice and be glad in it.
—Psalm 118:24

Chatting with God

Thank you, God, for new days and new mornings. Help me to be happy just because you love me. Help me to greet each new day with eagerness and joy. In Jesus' name, amen.

Did You Know?

Ideal surf conditions on the north shore of Kauai usually occur from November to March.

Devotion 70
Obeying Parents

Parents come in all shapes and sizes. Some
kids have one parent, others have two,
and some have several. But no matter what
combo of parents you have, God has given you
parents for a purpose. And as much as some of
us may think they are here to make our lives miserable, that's not what God had in mind.

My parents are the greatest. I am forever
thankful to God for them. They supported me and
encouraged me through the whole shark-attack
thing. I trust them and take their advice about my
present and my future. I listen to them because they
have been through a lot and help me make good
decisions.

Obeying our parents is what God expects
from us. When we obey our parents, we are
obeying God. It is so important that he
included it as one of the Ten Commandments
(Exodus 20). "Children, obey your parents
in everything, for this pleases the Lord"
(Colossians 3:20).

I am trying to please God every
day, so I am going to make sure to

obey him by obeying my parents. Will you
join me?

God's Words Inspire

*Children, obey your parents in the Lord, for
this is right. "Honor your father and mother" —
which is the first commandment with a promise
— "that it may go well with you and that you may
enjoy long life on the earth."*
—Ephesians 6:1–3

Chatting with God

Dear God, thank you for my parents. Bless them
in all that they do. Make them wise to know how
best to help me. Help me to respect them and to
obey them. In Jesus' name, amen.

Did You Know?

My parents have been surfing since they
were teenagers. My dad was on the East
Coast in New Jersey. My mom was on the West
Coast in California. They both came to Hawaii
looking for bigger and better waves, and that is
how they met.

Devotion 71

A Special Kind of Kindness

Have you ever wondered how you're supposed to treat somebody who has been mean to you? When we get hurt, we usually want to get back at whoever hurt us. But that's not what God tells us to do. God says that we should treat others with kindness—all the time. Even when somebody does something bad to us, we shouldn't take revenge.

We need to forgive others like God has forgiven us for all the junk we've done in our lives. "Make sure that nobody pays back wrong for wrong, but always try to be kind to each other and to everyone else" (1 Thessalonians 5:15).

There's a story about showing kindness to your enemies in 2 Samuel 9. King David wanted to find someone of Saul's family to be kind to. (Saul was the king who tried to kill David a couple of times.) David found a crippled man who was Saul's grandson. Although David was king and this man was poor, David did what

God wanted him to do—showered this man with kindness.

It's hard to be nice to mean people. But it's the right thing to do. And it's what God expects us to do since he did it for us.

God's Words Inspire

Be kind and compassionate to one another, forgiving each other, just as in Christ God forgave you.
—Ephesians 4:32

Chatting with God

Dear Lord, thank you for the kindness you have shown me. Fill me with your love so that I will be kind to others. When I want to get even with someone, remind me that I need to forgive and to show kindness instead. In Jesus' name, amen.

Did You Know?

The kindness rule in surfing is to not "drop in" on someone. That means if someone else has caught a wave, you don't cut in front of them and ride the wave yourself.

Devotion 72
Being Responsible

Life is full of responsibilities. We have responsibilities around the house, at school, to our friends, and for the special interests we have. When we get jobs, we'll be responsible for even more things. We are responsible for our actions and thoughts no matter where we are or who's watching.

I'm sure people think that because I get to travel and appear on TV I get special privileges or something. Not always! I still have work and chores just like everybody else. Doing all the traveling just means that when I am home I have to catch up. When my stay in the hospital cut into my normal schedule, I had loads of extra catching up to do. When I travel, I have responsibilities too. I need to be on time, be prepared, be flexible, and have a good attitude. God has handed me these additional responsibilities, and I can do them with his help.

You have responsibilities to your school, to your parents, and to God. Whatever responsibilities God sends your way, do them well. Do them gladly for Jesus.

God's Words Inspire

Whatever you do, work at it with all your heart, as working for the Lord, not for men.
—Colossians 3:23

Chatting with God

Dear God, thank you for giving me tasks to do. Help me to handle my responsibilities without complaining. I want to do everything the best I can and gladly. Everything I do, I do for you, Jesus. In Jesus' name, amen.

Did You Know?

A surfer's stance on the surfboard places him or her into one of two categories. A *natural* (or *regular*) *foot* is a surfer who puts the left foot forward. *A goofy foot* is a surfer who puts the right foot forward. (I'm a *goofy foot*.)

Devotion 73
Faith for Now

Jesus liked kids. He talked to children, held them on his lap, and hugged them. He even told the adults that they needed to behave more like children. He said that the kingdom of God belonged to the children.

So you know how little kids will climb onto something, yell "Daddy, catch!" and then jump off of it, knowing Daddy will be there to catch. That's the kind of faith God wants us to have in him. We just jump, knowing that he will catch us.

If God asks you to do something—like teach a Bible study—it can be a scary thing. But knowing that God will be there to back you up can give you faith to do what he asks without second thoughts.

You obviously won't know how to do everything from the start, but that is the fun part. The Holy Spirit will teach and guide you and speak through you. So you really have nothing to worry about. Just have that childlike faith.

God's Words Inspire

I tell you the truth, unless you change and become like little children, you will never enter the kingdom of heaven. Therefore, whoever humbles himself like this child is the greatest in the kingdom of heaven. And whoever welcomes a little child like this in my name welcomes me.
—Matthew 18:3–5

Chatting with God

Dear Jesus, thank you for loving kids. Thank you for loving me just the way I am right now. Help me to love you more each day. Make my faith in you grow and become stronger. In Jesus' name, amen.

Did You Know?

Hawaii is made up of 132 islands scattered over 1,523 miles of ocean. There are eight major islands: Oahu, Hawaii, Maui, Kauai (where I live), Lanai, Molokai, Nihau, and Kahoolawe.

Devotion 74
Willing Worship

I've always liked going to church. My church is the North Shore Community Church, and I enjoy going. It's great that my parents and my brothers attend church too, but I'd go even without them because I want to be close to God.

If you have a best friend, you know that you're always eager to spend time over at her house. Well, that's how it feels spending time with God at his house. God is the very best friend you could ever have. King David said, "I rejoiced with those who said to me, 'Let us go to the house of the Lord'" (Psalm 122:1). I love King David's attitude about worshiping God. He was excited about it. He wanted to be near to God in God's house. Thinking about how good God is makes me want to worship him, not only at church, but in my everyday life.

Going to church is just one of the opportunities we get to worship God. We can worship him wherever we are. We can thank him and praise him for who he is and what he does anytime and anywhere.

God's Words Inspire

Shout for joy to the LORD, all the earth. Worship the LORD with gladness; come before him with joyful songs ... Enter his gates with thanksgiving and his courts with praise; give thanks to him and praise his name. For the LORD is good and his love endures forever.

—Psalm 100:1–2, 4–5

Chatting with God

Dear God, I praise and thank you for being my God. Thank you for making it easy to go to church and worship you. Forgive me if I have not always been happy about going to church. Help me to be eager and willing to meet you at your house. I love you, Father. In Jesus' name, amen.

Did You Know?

More than fifty movies have been made on the island of Kauai, using Kauai's lush green scenery as the background. Some of the movies you may know are: *Hook, George of the Jungle, Jurassic Park,* and *King Kong.*

Devotion 75
Like Talking to a Friend

Some people find it hard to pray, so they come up with all kinds of excuses: "I don't know what to say." "I sound all goofy and dumb." "People will laugh if I don't do it right." God tells us that we shouldn't be anxious about anything, including prayer. Praying to God should be as easy as talking to your friends on your cell phone or by IM. Think of it as chatting with God. He won't laugh at you. Nothing you can ask of God in prayer is too silly or too small. He will listen when we ask for help. He will listen when we are sick or in pain. He will listen when we are afraid. He will listen when we pray for others. He will listen as we praise him and thank him.

It doesn't matter how you pray. Sometimes you will pray for a long time; other times it will be short. Sometimes you'll pray out loud; other times in your thoughts. Some prayers you'll say eloquently; others will come out choppy. God hears all prayers no matter how they are expressed. He listens lovingly and attentively when we talk to him.

God's Words Inspire

Do not be anxious about anything, but in everything, by prayer and petition, with thanksgiving, present your requests to God.
—Philippians 4:6

Chatting with God

Dear God, thank you for listening to everything I have to say. Thank you for not laughing when I talk to you—even if it doesn't come out quite right. Let me eagerly come to you with whatever is on my mind. In Jesus' name, amen.

Did You Know?

Soup is more than something hot you have for lunch. It's a surfing term for the white foam of the wave after the wave has broken.

Devotion 76
Giving Back to God

Everything we have comes from God. Our talents, health, and strength are gifts from God. His blessings let us live in a peaceful country where there is an abundance of food, jobs, and safety. We take gifts like the sun and the rain for granted—just because they've always been around. God continues to send gifts and blessings every day.

In thanks to God for everything he has given us, we need to give something back to him. Many of us give tithes to our church by putting money in the collection plate. Some of us give back by giving of our time or sharing our talents to help others.

I was just in Brazil for a surfing contest, and I met a girl from Tahiti who was really nice. Her surfboard, however, was not. It was old and pretty banged up. Her family couldn't afford to buy her a new one. So I prayed about it and felt like God wanted me to give her one of mine. So I did. Giving to those in need is one way to give back to God.

God's Words Inspire

Each man should give what he has decided in his heart to give, not reluctantly or under compulsion, for God loves a cheerful giver.
— 2 Corinthians 9:7

Chatting with God

Dear God, thank you for all you have given me. Everything I have comes from you. I want to give back to you what I can, either with money, my time, or through sharing with others. I am open to whatever you want me to do, and I will do it gladly. In Jesus' name, amen.

Did You Know?

A *quiver* is a surfer's collection of surfboards.

Devotion 77
No More Pity Party

Everybody has times when they feel sorry for themselves. You know, you want to hide in your room, throw yourself on the bed, and mope around. And when you come out, you want everyone else to feel bad for you too.

Having this kind of attitude hurts you more than anyone else. I was on a trip with my family once, and I complained and grumbled the entire time we were gone. The day was miserable for me. Gosh, how dumb it was of me not to enjoy that adventure and time with my family.

So now, when things are not going my way, I will try to remember Philippians 2:14 and change my mind-set:

1. I'll stop thinking about myself.

2. I'll focus on the good things that are happening and the great opportunities I may have.

3. I'll find something that I can do for somebody else and then do it.

It's normal to be down every once in a while, but don't stay there, and try not to complain about it. God has done great things for you. Remember those things and focus on the good that is to come.

God's Words Inspire

Do everything without complaining or arguing
—Philippians 2:14

Chatting with God

Dear God, forgive me for complaining and feeling sorry for myself. When I'm down, help me to turn to you for help to cheer me up. Remind me that I have so many things to be thankful for and to be happy about. Give me courage to get on with it and stop thinking about myself. In Jesus' name, amen.

Did You Know?

A *luau* in Hawaii is a big party! *Luaus* usually feature roasted pig, rice, fish, and other local dishes, lots of singing, music, and dancing. Enjoy one if you ever visit the islands.

Devotion 78
Stuff Happens

Sometimes the unexpected happens.
Your parents separate, a disaster hits your
town, a family member becomes very ill, your
grandma dies, or you or a friend get seriously
injured. Nobody wants to face these things.
They hurt, really bad, really deep. The shark
attack was definitely unexpected for me and my
family and friends. Nobody expected a shark would
attack and change my life (and the lives of my family
as well). But the unexpected did happen.
Dealing with an unexpected change in our lives
takes strength. It takes a lot of courage to pick up
and move on. Your family and friends will help
you find some of the strength you will need. But
you will need more than they can offer. God has
enough strength and courage for all of us. He
supplied me with the strength to keep going,
and he can do the same for you.
The Bible tells us that "God causes
everything to work together for the good
of those who love God and are called
according to his purpose for them"
(Romans 8:28 NLT). You can be

sure that even if everything is turned upside down in your life at the moment, God is working it all out and you can be okay with God in charge.

God's Words Inspire

Be strong and courageous. Do not be afraid or discouraged .... with us is the LORD our God to help us and to fight our battles.
                    —2 Chronicles 32:7, 8

Chatting with God

God, it is scary when something upsets my normal life. Allow me to feel your strength. Give me courage to face what happens. Help me to get through those times. In Jesus' name, amen.

Did You Know?

The island of Kauai has a population of 60,000 people (not including tourists).

Devotion 79
Extra Helpers

There are a bunch of people in my life, besides my parents, who are helping me do all that I need to do. I respect all these people because I know they will help me reach my goals and see my dreams come true.

Russell Lewis and Ben Aipa are my surfing coaches. Russell helped me develop my style, and Ben helped me adjust to surfing with one arm. They are great at coming up with ideas for solving any problem. Roy Hofstetter is my agent. He helps manage all the requests and opportunities that come my way. He's great at sorting through everything and then asking what I'm most interested in doing.

Becky Baumgartner, my assistant, helps me answer emails and do interviews and other things. My brothers, Noah and Timmy, help me with any computer, photography, or video questions I have. They also, along with my dad, help me with my surfing.

You have a lot of special people in your life too: coaches, teachers, youth leaders, friends, and family. These people are all tools that God is using to mold and shape you, and they deserve your respect, kindness, and gratitude.

God's Words Inspire

Two are better than one, because they have a good return for their work: If one falls down, his friend can help him up.
— Ecclesiastes 4:9–10

Chatting with God

Dear God, thank you for all the people in my life who encourage and help me through each day. Help me to always be respectful and kind. In Jesus' name, amen.

Did You Know?

The surf conditions in Hawaii vary because of storms out in the Pacific Ocean during different seasons. But one thing's for sure: the water temperature is always warm. The average temperature is seventy-four degrees in the winter and eighty degrees in the summer!

Devotion 80
Everything Sings Praise

Singing praise songs to God is one of my favorite things about going to church. I really like contemporary music with a great beat that makes you want to stand up, move your feet, and clap your hands. God enjoys all kinds of music and singing. The type of music and song that we praise him with is not as important as doing it from our hearts.

All kinds of creatures "sing" their praise to God. Everything that God created praises him when they do what he made them to do: birds soar, dolphins play, cranes dance, wolves howl, the sun and moon follow their paths, the angels rejoice, and the snow lies over the dormant earth.

God is almighty. He is greater than anything in the universe. And he loves us no matter what we do. He forgives us. He cares for us. He protects and guides us. He gives us great gifts—everything from rain to families. All these things make him worthy of our praise.

Do you breathe? Then you were made to praise God. "Praise the Lord. How good it is to sing praises to our God, how pleasant and fitting to praise him!" (Psalm 147:1).

God's Words Inspire

Let everything that has breath praise the LORD. Praise the LORD.
—Psalm 150:6

Chatting with God

Almighty God, I praise you for all you are. I praise you for your wonderful creation. I praise you for all you have done for me. Let me gladly praise your name for ever and ever. In Jesus' name, amen.

Did You Know?

The Hawaiian honeycreeper, or 'i'iwi, is a bird (about the size of a sparrow) that lives only in Hawaii. It got its name from how it creeps when searching flowers for nectar and insects.

Devotion 81
Super Joy

My life is full of joy. I am joyful because I am able to do things that thrill me, including surfing. I am joyful because I have parents and brothers and friends who love me. I am joyful because I live in one of the most beautiful places on earth—Kauai. But most of all I am joyful because God is with me. He is my strength. He is my salvation. He is my joy.

People often write to me asking me why I am so joyful, so happy. It's not the celebrity status or my name in the headlines that bring me joy. It's God. God's love is what puts the joy in my life and the smile on my face.

When we have God in our lives, we are filled with a deep-down joy that is rock solid. Nobody and nothing can take that kind of joy away from us. People, things, and activities can bring us happiness, but not the lasting and unchanging joy that God brings us. Things can rot or break, people can disappoint us, activities will pass, but God never changes. He "is the same yesterday and today and forever" (Hebrews 13:8).

God's Words Inspire

The joy of the LORD is your strength.
—Nehemiah 8:10

Chatting with God

Dear God, thank you for being my joy. With you in my life I will always have deep-down joy that nobody can take away. Thank you for filling my life with joy even when things don't go well. I praise you for this life-long joy. In Jesus' name, amen.

Did You Know?

Most surfers have more than one surfboard. They'll choose the board to use depending on the size and shape of the waves and how they want to surf those waves. Long boards are about seven to nine feet long. And short boards are less than seven feet long.

Devotion 82
Mouth Checkup

What's coming out of your mouth? Are you more careful about the way you talk if your mother is in the room? Do you watch what you say when your pastor is there? What if God was standing right behind you? What then? I bet you would be extra careful and think before you opened your mouth. Well, I have some news. God IS right behind you. God is everywhere, so he hears what you're saying. He knows when you trash somebody verbally. He knows when you use his name disrespectfully. He knows when you lie. He even knows when you *think* the words but catch yourself before you say them.

If your language has gotten sloppy and your thoughts trashy, then it's time to clean it up. God has given us some good instructions on what not to say: First, "You shall not misuse the name of the LORD your God, for the LORD will not hold anyone guiltless who misuses his name" (Exodus 20:7). Second, "If you keep your mouth shut, you will stay out of trouble" (Proverbs 21:23 NLT). Third, "The LORD detests lying lips" (Proverbs 12:22). Fourth, "Now you must rid yourselves of all such things as these: anger, rage, malice, slander, and filthy language from your lips" (Colossians 3:8).

Those are the basics, straight from God. It's time for a mouth checkup.

God's Words Inspire

May the words of my mouth and the meditation on my heart be pleasing in your sight, O LORD, my Rock and my Redeemer.
                                                    —Psalm 19:14

Chatting with God

Oh Lord, forgive me for saying unkind things about others. Forgive me for swearing and using your name wrong. May all my words and all my thoughts bring honor and glory to you. In Jesus' name, amen.

Did You Know?

The Hawaiian alphabet has only 12 letters: A, E, H, I, K, L, M, N, O, P, U, W. Every Hawaiian word and syllable ends in a vowel.

Devotion 83
A Rainbow of Promises

God's promises come in as many varieties as the colors in a rainbow. They are scattered throughout the Bible. They give us hope and peace. My very favorite promise (as you know) is the one in Jeremiah 29:11 about God's plans for our future. Check it out in your Bible. It's awesome! It's hard for us to keep even the simplest promises we make. We promise to keep a secret, and then we pass on the news. We promise to clean our room on Saturday, and then we go out with a friend. We promise to email someone tonight, and then we forget. We make our promises very casually.

But God takes his promises seriously. The Bible says, "The Lord is faithful to all his promises" (Psalm 145:13). God keeps his promises through generations of people over thousands of years. When God promised Noah that he would never flood the earth again, he sent a rainbow as the sign of the promise. So the next time you see a rainbow, remember that God's promises are for us today.

God's Words Inspire

As long as the earth endures, seedtime and harvest, cold and heat, summer and winter, day and night will never cease.
—Genesis 8:22

Chatting with God

Dear Lord, thank you for all your promises. Thank you for keeping them. Help me to take the promises I make to others more seriously. In Jesus' name, amen.

Did You Know?

There are rainbows almost every day on Kauai! They are so beautiful! Sometimes rainbows double or triple up or extend to be full circles!

Devotion 84
Mixed Messages

Every day we are bombarded with hundreds of messages from magazines, radio, TV, and the Internet. Some messages can inspire us or help us grow. Some messages can do the opposite and confuse us as to what is right. They can make us think that sexually explicit material is okay to look at. That swearing is cool. That breaking the law can make us popular. These messages pollute our minds. Some people think that violent or degrading images or swearing won't affect them. They blind themselves with excuses: "This one time won't hurt." Or, "I can handle it and just forget it." Or, "It's not like I haven't seen it before!" It doesn't matter how strong you are, everything that we expose our brains to affects us.

Feeding our brains with trash will cause garbage to seep into our lives, fill our thoughts, and spill out through our mouths and actions. And like a sewage spill, it won't go unnoticed by God and others.

To follow God's way, we need to stay in touch every day with God by reading the Bible, having devotions, and talking to God through prayer. By feeding our brains God food, we won't fall into the trap of following the mixed messages of the world.

God's Words Inspire

Do not conform any longer to the pattern of this world, but be transformed by the renewing of your mind. Then you will be able to test and approve what God's will is—his good, pleasing and perfect will.
—Romans 12:2

Chatting with God

Dear God, thank you for giving me clear guidelines in the Bible. Thank you for your Word that provides me with healthy brain food. Let it renew my mind. Help me to avoid the negative messages of the world and to follow your true messages instead. In Jesus' name, amen.

Did You Know?

Wahine is the Hawaiian word for "woman." In surfing lingo the same word means "female surfer."

Devotion 85
Sticking Out

Most of us prefer to blend in with the crowd. We prefer to go unnoticed rather than be seen as different. I used to think that, but I obviously stick out from the rest of my surfing buddies now. Anybody can spot the "one-arm surfer" in the water. I'm pretty hard to miss. But it actually doesn't bother me.

We also like to fit in with our friends by the way we talk or the way we act. Depending on who you hang with, this might not be too big a problem. But if you are a Christian and the friends you have aren't, you need to be careful how you "fit in."

We are God's people. We are holy. God has declared us holy because of Jesus. The Bible says that we need to keep growing in holiness. We might stick out and be different than other people because we are living godly lives— but that's a good thing. If people notice that we act differently and talk differently than everybody else, they will see that Jesus lives in our lives and hearts.

God's Words Inspire

*What kind of people ought you to be? You
ought to live holy and godly lives as you look
forward to the day of God and speed its coming.*
—2 Peter 3:11–12

Chatting with God

Dear God, thank you for calling me to be one
of your people—to be holy. Help me to stick out in a
good way. Help me to show others that you live in me
and that I belong to you. In Jesus' name, amen.

Did You Know?

If someone in Hawaii calls you a *haole*, it
means they can tell you are not a local. *Haole*
means "white person (Caucasian) or foreigner."

Devotion 86
Let's Be Honest

People aren't always honest. Have you heard someone say, "Your new haircut looks nice" and then turn away and laugh with a friend? You knew right away that she was lying.

Sometimes you might think you can't tell your friend the whole truth, like when she gets braces and asks you, "Do these make me look weird? I feel like I look funny with braces." But what exactly are you supposed to say? That can be hard—to be honest without hurting your friend's feelings.

Honesty can be a tricky thing. You may think you can escape trouble if you just tell part of the truth. But usually it doesn't work. Your parents or teachers may catch on when the details don't add up. Or your friends may compare notes, and then there's a bigger mess to get yourself out of. The Bible says, "The truth will set you free" (John 8:32).

We all need to practice being honest. It may seem easier to tell a little white lie, but it probably isn't. Like the Bible says, "An honest answer is like a warm hug" (Proverbs 24:26 THE MESSAGE). That's a cool comparison! Let's practice spreading the truth. Let's pass around those warm hugs.

God's Words Inspire

"These are the things you are to do: Speak the truth to each other, and render true and sound judgment in your courts; do not plot evil against your neighbor, and do not love to swear falsely. I hate all this," declares the LORD.
—Zechariah 8:16–17

Chatting with God

Dear Jesus, forgive me for not always telling the truth. Help me to be honest. Make me wise to know what to say so that I always give out "warm hugs" with my words. In Jesus' name, amen.

Did You Know?

A *ding* is a cut, crack, or nick on the surface of your surfboard. A lie is like a ding in your reputation.

Devotion 87

We've Got the Power

Sometimes when I have the chance to talk about Jesus to others, I get all shy about it. I worry about what I'll say or what the people will think about me after I've said it. If I know I have to speak to a whole group of people, I practice what I'm going to say first. But when I don't have time to think about it, I say a little prayer that Jesus will give me the right words. I also ask that I have the courage to say it. And then the right words just seem to come out. The more I do this, the easier it is to talk about Jesus to others.

When we become Christians, God fills us with his Spirit. The Bible says that God is strong and mighty. His Spirit is powerful. When we have faith, we have that same power within us to say and do great things for God. We have the power to love others, to do what is right, and to do what pleases God. Telling others about Jesus is one of the best things we can do to please God.

God's Words Inspire

For God did not give us a spirit of timidity, but a spirit of power, of love and of self-discipline.
                    —2 Timothy 1:7

Chatting with God

Dear God, thank you for filling me with your Spirit of power. Help me to be strong and have the courage to talk about you to others. Let your love shine through me in everything I do and say. In Jesus' name, amen.

Did You Know?

A surfboard has several parts. The deck is the top of the board. The nose is the pointy front end. The rails are the sides. The fins are on the bottom. Some boards have one fin; others have two or three.

Devotion 88
Armor of God

Unfortunately the world is full of sin. Ever since Adam and Eve disobeyed God in the garden of Eden, there has been sin in the world. Jesus came to earth and saved us from our sin, but it's still hanging around.

The urge to sin is within us. We are tempted by all kinds of messages: Try this. Buy this. You must have ... You'll be cool if ... Sin is like the big bad wolf. It's knocking at our door all the time yelling at us, "Let me come in."

That's kind of a scary thought. But there's good news—we don't have to fight off sin on our own. God is on our side. He is strong and mighty and provides us with equipment—our armor of protection. Our protection looks like this: a belt of truth, a breastplate of righteousness, a shield of faith, a helmet of salvation, and the sword of the Spirit (Ephesians 6:10–18).

With that kind of protection and God by our side, we will be ready to face anything. For sure we can overcome any temptation that comes our way.

God's Words Inspire

God is faithful; he will not let you be tempted beyond what you can bear. But when you are tempted, he will also provide a way out so that you can stand up under it.
                    —1 Corinthians 10:13

Chatting with God

Dear God, thank you for your protection. Thank you for giving me the armor I need to help me fight off sin. Make me strong in your Word and in your power to say no to sin. In Jesus' name, amen.

Did You Know?

A *surf leash* is a long plastic cord with a Velcro strap at one end (that goes around your ankle) to attach you to your surfboard. This way you don't lose your board in rough water or when you wipe out.

Devotion 89

Getting to Know You

Our lives can be awfully busy. They are filled with good things like school and homework, flute lessons and play practice, friendships and roller skating parties, sleepovers and gymnastics. But sometimes we're just rushing from one activity to the next. Sometimes we get so busy with all this stuff we need to do, that we forget to take the time to be with God.

God wants to be your friend. He wants to spend time with you. But it's up to you to find the time in your busy day to spend time with him. You need to take the time to be quiet, to read the Bible, and to talk to God. If you take the time to really learn God's Word, you will find out that we are privileged to live in a very special time. Each of us has been handpicked by God for such a time as this! The Bible says, "Be still before the LORD and wait patiently for him" (Psalm 37:7). We need to be quiet and we need to be patient in order to get to know him.

God is waiting for us. We just have to slow down long enough to spend time with him.

God's Words Inspire

Be still, and know that I am God; I will be exalted among the nations, I will be exalted in the earth.
—Psalm 46:10

Chatting with God

Dear God, thank you for letting us know you. Thank you for being a mighty and powerful God. Help me to be still and spend time with you in quiet so I can get to know you better. In Jesus' name, amen.

Did You Know?

There are over 2.5 million surfers in the United States alone. Men have been surfing for ages. Women's surfing got really popular during the 1990s and has become even more popular in the past few years.

Devotion 90
Into the Future

Sometimes it's scary. Sometimes it's really exciting. The future lies ahead, and we have no idea what it will bring. Some people are so eager to know what the future holds that they go to fortune-tellers or read their horoscopes. But those things are worthless. God wants us to trust him alone for our future. It might have some ups and downs, some surprises and unexpected turns, but God will be in control no matter what. And his love for us is unfailing and never ending!

I don't know exactly what I'll be doing in the future. But I do know that I will continue to stay close to God. With God as my guide, I know I can do anything that he inspires me to do. Maybe I'll continue on to be a professional surfer. Maybe I'll become a great speaker or a photographer. Who knows? Anything is possible. God could have ideas that are bigger than anything I can imagine right now. Maybe I'll discover new talents that I've never known before. You might too.

No one knows exactly what the future holds. But there is one thing I do know: God is on my side (Psalm 56:9).

God's Words Inspire

For I am convinced that neither death nor life, neither angels nor demons, neither the present nor the future, nor any powers, neither height nor depth, nor anything else in all creation, will be able to separate us from the love of God that is in Christ Jesus our Lord.

—Romans 8:38–39

Chatting with God

Dear God, thank you for planning my future. Thank you for your love that surrounds me every day. Stay close by my side. Lead me into the future you have planned just for me. In Jesus' name, amen.

Did You Know?

I've surfed in many different places all over the world: Australia, New Zealand, Brazil, Samoa, Nicaragua, California, and New Jersey. But my favorite place is Pine Trees in Hanalei Bay on Kauai. It is my "homebreak."

Ask Bethany

FAQs: Surfing, Faith & Friends

*Bethany Hamilton
with Doris Rikkers*

Honest, sometimes gut-wrenching questions from Bethany Hamilton's fan mail—paired with inspirational Bible verses and Bethany's own answers—will keep girls ages eight to twelve turning the pages of this book.

Available in stores and online!

Soul Surfer Bible
With Bethany Hamilton

A companion to the Soul Surfer books, this NIV surfer-style Bible helps girls eight to twelve apply Bethany Hamilton's messages of courage, hope, and faith. This Bible includes twelve full-color inserts that will help teens apply Bethany's mission to their own lives.

Italian Duo-Tone™, Glitter Wave

Available in stores and online!

ZONDERVAN®
.com

We want to hear from you. Please send your comments about this book to us in care of zreview@zondervan.com. Thank you.